HIKING WYOMING'S BIGHORN MOUNTAINS

HELP US KEEP THIS GUIDE UP TO DATE

Every effort has been made by the author and editors to make this guide as accurate and useful as possible. However, many things may change after a guide is published—trails may be rerouted, regulations may change, techniques may evolve, facilities may come under new management, etc.

We would appreciate hearing from you concerning your experiences with this guide and how you feel it could be improved and kept up to date. While we may not be able to respond to all comments and suggestions, we'll take them to heart, and we'll also make certain to share them with the authors. Please send your comments and suggestions to the following address:

Globe Pequot
Reader Response/Editorial Department
246 Goose Lane
Guilford, CT 06437

Or you may e-mail us at: editorial@falcon.com

Thanks for your input, and happy trails!

HIKING WYOMING'S
BIGHORN MOUNTAINS

A GUIDE TO THE AREA'S GREATEST HIKING ADVENTURES

Ken Keffer

GUILFORD, CONNECTICUT

To the members of the Outdoor Writers Association of America. You are truly the voice of the outdoors. I've learned much from you all.

FALCONGUIDES®

An imprint of Globe Pequot
Falcon and FalconGuides are registered trademarks and Make Adventure Your Story is a trademark of Rowman & Littlefield.

Distributed by NATIONAL BOOK NETWORK

Copyright © 2017 Rowman & Littlefield
TOPO! Maps copyright © 2017 National Geographic Partners, LLC. All Rights Reserved.
Maps by Melissa Baker © Rowman & Littlefield

All images by Ken Keffer unless otherwise credited

British Library Cataloguing in Publication Information available

Library of Congress Cataloging-in-Publication Data available

ISBN 978-1-4930-2227-4 (paperback)
ISBN 978-1-4930-2228-1 (e-book)

♾ The paper used in this publication meets the minimum requirements of American National Standard for Information Sciences—Permanence of Paper for Printed Library Materials, ANSI/NISO Z39.48-1992.

The author and Rowman & Littlefield assume no liability for accidents happening to, or injuries sustained by, readers who engage in the activities described in this book.

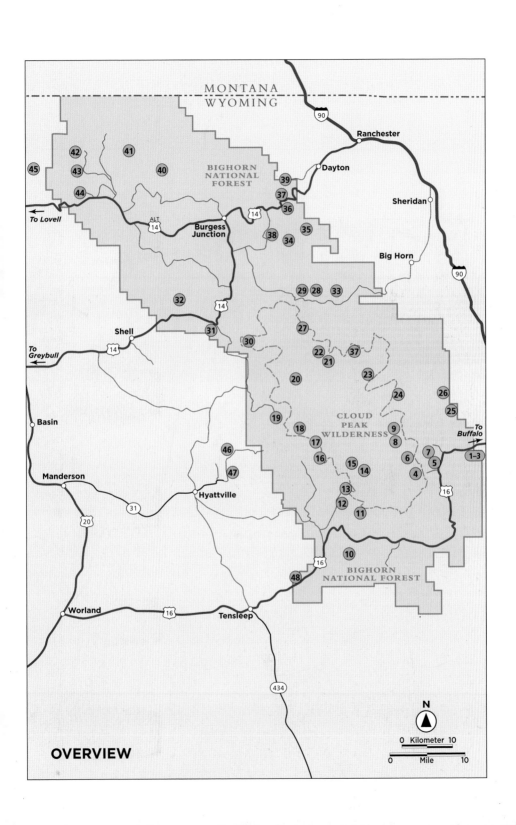

OVERVIEW

Bighorns in the fall
LINDA LULIAS

THE HIKES

ACKNOWLEDGMENTS

I'd like to give a special acknowledgment to the staff of the United States Forest Service. With a mandate for multiple uses, the Forest Service is held to the impossible standard of making everyone happy all of the time. Thank you all for doing your thankless jobs and for doing them well. The employees of the Bighorn National Forest deserve the utmost respect. I've been a user of the forest for nearly four decades, and every staff member I've ever encountered has been pleasant and helpful. I'd like to give Sara Evans Kirol and Donna Wilson extra props, as they were heavily involved as I gathered information for the writing of this guidebook.

Many other folks also provided nuggets of information that ultimately were helpful for this book. Thanks to all of the hikers, guides, travelers, and shopkeepers that offered up a suggestion or two. Your anonymous contributions were appreciated. I am also grateful to the staff at the Bureau of Land Management, Wyoming State Parks, and the Bighorn Canyon National Recreation Area for providing assistance. The Backcountry Horsemen of America's Cloud Peak Chapter is a volunteer group that is responsible for miles of trail work each season. Everyone who hikes the Bighorns should recognize their dedication and efforts.

The FalconGuides team at Rowman & Littlefield also deserves kudos. My personal collection of FalconGuides has always been extensive and well worn. I'm honored to now have my own title under this umbrella of guidebooks.

Dr. Uwe Stender of Triada US Literary Agency has become more than my agent. I rely heavily on him for guidance and mentorship in the publishing realm.

I have a special connection with the Bighorn Mountains, and I owe much of this to my extended family. Both the Keffer and the Ritchie clans are from the Buffalo area, and my kinfolk take up a large section of the Johnson County phonebook. I've got endless memories of Bighorn adventures with my relatives. My entire family helped shape my childhood, and I hope I can pass on a few of the lessons I learned in nature from them. Pa put in lots of miles specifically for this book, and Grandma Keffer basically ran a bed and breakfast for me as I researched the trails.

Heather Ray has been my unwavering support for a number of years. She always has the words of encouragement to pick me up when I'm down. She is always the first to congratulate me when I am up. She gives the best hugs always. She's also an excellent writer and editor, and this publication is far superior because of her talents.

Scott Schaefer, Dusty Evenson, and Justin Kahle all deserve a mention, if for no other reason than the summer of 1998. We trekked lot of miles in the Bighorns that year. I'm glad we still get to make new memories on occasion. More recently, Jarren, Tara, and Bray Kuipers were all very helpful in their own ways. Also thanks to Jodie Atherton for sharing Kirk VanDyke with me for a memorable weekend of fishing and hiking the Bighorns.

Thanks to everyone who contributed photos, including Charles Hubbell, Tim Feathers, Molly McKay, and Aunt Linda Lulias. Rohy Keffer took some photos, hiked some trails, reported on some roads, and ran many shuttles for me. Thanks, Pa.

Erik Molvar's *Hiking Cloud Peak Wilderness* was a helpful resource. Bill Hunger's *Hiking Wyoming* and Kenneth Graham's *Fishing Wyoming* were also references I consulted often. I relied heavily on Brett Prettyman's expertise for this project as well.

I have been blessed with some amazing mentors. Special thanks go to Paul and Mary Lussow for always welcoming me with an open cabin. Your backyard trees provide an ideal hammock-pitching spot, and your wireless internet saved me a few trips down the mountain.

I dedicate Hike #48, Salt Lick Trail, to Mark Winland and Gwyn McKee. I thought about you both often as I wandered the mountains, but never more than when I was hiking up the side of Tensleep Canyon. I miss the hell out of you, Mark. I admire the hell out of you, Gwyn.

MEET YOUR GUIDE

Ken Keffer was born at the base of the Bighorn Mountains in Buffalo, Wyoming, and he already has his burial plot paid for at the local cemetery (Block 15, Lot 14, Space 3). He received a wildlife biology degree from the University of Wyoming.

ROHY KEFFER

KEN KEFFER'S TOP 5 HIKING TIPS

5. **Take an Umbrella.** I learned this tip from Continental Divide Trail thru-hikers. An umbrella keeps the rain and the sun off of you. You can use it to block the breeze when you light a camp stove, too.

4. **Try Tenkara Fly-Fishing.** Tenkara is only a rod and line, no reel. There are plenty of fishing opportunities in the Bighorns, and Tenkara doesn't take up much space in a pack.

3. **Try Snowshoeing.** It's basically hiking in the winter. The woods are extra peaceful under a blanket of snow. You can rent a pair and try it, or you can buy a decent pair for fairly cheap.

2. **You Don't Need Boots.** For the most part, normal tennis shoes are fine for hiking. Flip-flops aren't a great idea, but there are plenty of great sturdy sandals that make fine footwear. Lightweight and comfortable, works best for me.

1. **Be Kind to Your Feet.** Pamper them even, before and after hiking. Pack an extra pair of socks or three. Changing socks midday is a lightweight luxury. Peel off your socks the instant you get to camp. Hiking is hard on your feet; don't neglect them.

He has authored numerous books connecting families to nature, including *The Kids' Outdoor Adventure Book* (Winner of a 2013 National Outdoor Book Award Honorable Mention), *The Truth About Nature,* and *The Secret Lives of Animals.* Additionally, he penned *Ranger Rick: National Parks!* as well as two outdoor nature activity journals: *We Love Nature* and *Bird Brainiacs.* More information about Ken's work can be found at www.kenkeffer.net.

A vagabond naturalist and environmental educator, Ken has worked in Wyoming, Alaska, Maryland, New Mexico, Ohio, Wisconsin, and the Gobi Desert of Mongolia. Ken enjoys floating on lazy rivers, birding, snowshoeing, fly-fishing, and walking his dogs, Willow the Wonder Mutt and Hazel the Wonder Nut.

HOW TO USE THE MAPS

The maps in this book that depict a detailed close-up of an area use color to portray relief. These maps will give you a good idea of elevation gain and loss. They are a good reference, but should not replace United States Geological Survey (USGS) Topographic maps that should be used as the navigational tool.

Map and Icon Legends

ICON LEGEND

 BEST
FOR PHOTOS

 HIKES FOR
FAMILIES

 HIKES FOR
WATERFALLS

 DOG-FRIENDLY
TRAILS

 FINDING
SOLITUDE

NOTES ON MAPS

Topographic maps are an essential companion to the activities in this guide. Falcon has partnered with National Geographic to provide the best mapping resources. Each activity is accompanied by a detailed map and the name of the National Geographic TOPO! map (USGS),which can be downloaded for free from natgeomaps.com. If the activity takes place on a National Geographic Trails Illustrated map it will be noted. Continually setting the standard for accuracy, each Trails Illustrated topographic map is crafted in conjunction with local land managers and undergoes rigorous review and enhancement before being printed on waterproof, tear-resistant material. Trails Illustrated maps and information about their digital versions, that can be used on mobile GPS applications, can be found at natgeomaps.com.

MAP LEGEND

〔15〕	Interstate			National Park
〔93〕	US Highway		Ⓟ	Parking
〔28〕	State Highway		‿	Pass/Gap
〔250〕	County/Forest/Local Road		▲	Peak
▬ ▬ ▬	Featured Route on Trail		⊞	Picnic Area
▬▬▬▬	Featured Route on Road		▢	Point of Interest
▬▬▬▬	Featured Route on Unpaved Road		⊠	Quarry
- - - -	Trail			Ranger Station/Park Office
	Bench			Rapids
‿	Bridge		Ⓡ	Registration Box
▲	Backcountry Campground			Scenic View
	Boat Ramp			Shelter
	Cabin			Spring
△	Campground		①	Trailhead
•—•	Gate		?	Visitor/Information Center
	Inn/Lodging			Waterfall
	Mine			

	BEST PHOTOS	FAMILY FRIENDLY	WATER FEATURES	DOG FRIENDLY	FINDING SOLITUDE
BUFFALO & SOUTHEAST WILDERNESS ACCESS					
1. Grouse Mountain	•	•			
2. Mosier Gulch	•	•	•		
3. Clear Creek Trail		•	•	•	
4. Circle Park Loop	•	•			
5. Long Lake			•	•	
6. Lake Angeline			•	•	
7. Seven Brothers Lakes	•		•		
8. Florence Pass	•		•		
9. Ant Hill	•				•
POWDER RIVER PASS & WESTERN WILDERNESS ACCESS					
10. James T. Saban Lookout	•	•			
11. Lake McLain			•		•
12. Tensleep Trail		•	•	•	
13. Tensleep Falls	•	•	•		
14. Lost Twin Lakes	•		•		
15. Mistymoon Lake	•		•		
16. Middle Paint Rock Creek	•			•	
17. Lake Solitude Trail			•	•	
18. Poacher Lake	•		•		
19. Cliff Lake	•		•		

	BEST PHOTOS	FAMILY FRIENDLY	WATER FEATURES	DOG FRIENDLY	FINDING SOLITUDE
NORTHERN WILDERNESS ACCESS					
20. Edelman Pass	•		•		
21. Geneva Pass	•		•		
22. Rinehart Lakes		•	•		
23. Highland Park & Lake Winnie	•		•		
24. The Reservoirs	•		•		
25. Firebox Park				•	•
26. South Rock Creek	•		•		
RED GRADE TO SHELL					
27. Geddes Lake	•		•		
28. Sawmill Lakes		•	•	•	
29. Coney Lake				•	
30. Old Mail Trail		•		•	
31. Bench Trail	•			•	
32. Cedar Creek				•	•
NORTHEAST BIGHORNS					
33. Walker Prairie	•				
34. Wolf Creek			•		•
35. Wolf Creek Falls Overlook	•		•		
36. Horseshoe Mountain				•	•
37. Steamboat Point	•	•		•	
38. Black Mountain Lookout	•	•			
39. Tongue River Canyon	•	•	•	•	

	BEST PHOTOS	FAMILY FRIENDLY	WATER FEATURES	DOG FRIENDLY	FINDING SOLITUDE
MEDICINE WHEEL & SURROUNDINGS					
40. Bull Elk Park					•
41. Little Horn Trail			•	•	
42. Bucking Mule Falls	•		•		
43. Porcupine Falls	•		•		
44. Medicine Wheel	•	•			
45. Cottonwood Canyon		•		•	•
SOUTHWEST BIGHORNS & BASIN COUNTRY					
46. Medicine Lodge Archaeological Site	•	•			
47. Paint Rock Canyon Trail	•		•		
48. Salt Lick Trail	•				•

BEFORE YOU HIT THE TRAIL

OVERVIEW

An isolated range materializing out of the **Bighorn and Powder River Basins** of northern Wyoming, the Bighorn Mountains stand tall. Tucked in-between Yellowstone and the Black Hills, the Bighorns are at the crossroads of Interstates 25 and 90.

While sometimes overshadowed by Yellowstone, the Tetons, and the Wind River Mountains, the Bighorn Mountains are a popular regional destination, regularly drawing campers and hikers from the surrounding states, the Midwest, and throughout Wyoming. They are a bit of a hidden gem, since they are every bit as worthy of a destination as their more famous neighbors.

The Precambrian granite found at the core of the Bighorn Mountains is the oldest rock in the range, dating back 1 billion years. The Bighorns are a classic anticline, a massive upward bulging of the earth's crust, that occurred as continental land masses collided. The forces of the impact caused the bedrock to fold upward. The landscape has since been sculpted by eons of erosion. Streams coursing down the flanks cut through the sedimentary strata forming the deep canyons along the edges of the range. Between 50,000 and 8,000 years ago (quite recently in geologic time), the grinding action of glaciers sculpted the half-domes, sheer cliffs, and deep lake basins that are the hallmark of the Cloud Peak Wilderness.

Originally established as the Bighorn Forest Reserve in 1897, the Bighorn National Forest is 80 miles long and over 30 miles wide. The forest covers 1,115,073 acres and has over thirty campgrounds including four group campgrounds, ten picnic areas, eight lodges, multiple reservoirs, miles and miles of streams, and more

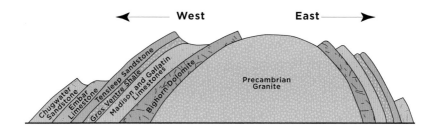

than 1,200 miles of trails. The Bighorns are clearly an outdoor recreation paradise. Hunting and fishing opportunities are top-notch (see Flora and Fauna). Hikers can find anything from a short day hike to the Solitude Loop Trail that runs more than 65 miles. A growing network of motorized trails can be found throughout the Bighorns as well.

Within the Bighorn National Forest is the Cloud Peak Wilderness. Known as the Cloud Peak Primitive Area as far back as 1932, the 189,039-acre area was declared wilderness in 1984.

The Bighorn Mountains truly offer something for every hiker. From short scenic day trips to extended multiple day backpacking excursions, *Hiking Wyoming's Bighorn Mountains* will highlight the essentials of the region. The book covers forty-eight trails in depth and mentions numerous additional hikes as alternatives. The hikes include lands of the Bighorn National Forest, the Cloud Peak Wilderness, and surrounding state and federal lands.

At over 170 miles long from north to south, the majority of the mountain range is administered by the US Forest Service as the Bighorn National Forest. The northern extent of the range crosses the Wyoming/Montana state line and is a part of the Crow Indian Reservation. The southern reaches are privately held.

Three major highways climb over the Bighorn Mountains. All three are official Scenic Byways offering up numerous scenic pullouts and interpretive displays along the routes. The Cloud Peak Skyway Scenic Byway (US Hwy. 16) connects Buffalo to the town of Ten Sleep. It crosses Powder River Pass and provides excellent views of Cloud Peak and surrounding mountains. Fields of wildflowers accent the views during the summer season. The route also passes through rugged Tensleep Canyon, an area growing in popularity with rock climbers.

The Bighorn Scenic Byway (US Hwy. 14) begins west of Sheridan near Dayton and Ranchester. It quickly climbs the eastern slopes of the mountain, reaching Burgess Junction, before descending through gorgeous Shell Canyon. This route passes Shell Falls Interpretive Site on the way to Greybull. Shell Falls is closed seasonally.

Closed in the winter, the Medicine Wheel Passage (US Hwy. Alternate 14) runs from Burgess Junction to Lovell and the Bighorn Basin to the west. The road grades are steep, so large vehicles should be aware and protect their brakes when heading down the mountain. The Medicine Wheel Passage passes mountain meadows, and is the access route for the Medicine Wheel/Medicine Mountain National Historic Landmark. The only National Recreation Trail in the region, Bucking Mule Falls, runs just north of this sacred site.

Although the Bighorn National Forest has a long history, things are always changing. Perhaps most exciting is when new trails are blazed. In 2016, for example, trail crews put in a new route, the Tensleep Trail (Hike 11), near the Island Park and Deer Park Campgrounds near West Tensleep Lake. This daytrip makes a great option for exploring a popular area of the forest.

WEATHER

The weather can be unpredictable in the Bighorn Mountains. The region is characterized by cool summers and snowy winters. Afternoon thunderstorms can materialize out of nowhere in the summer, quickly turning a sunny cloudless day into a drenching downpour. In most years, snow lingers until early June in many places. It doesn't snow in the high country every August, but it does with enough regularity that you have to be prepared for that possibility. One of my favorite Fourth of Julys was spent fishing in a blizzard with my cousin at Meadowlark Lake.

That said, the area gets an abundance of sunshine. Without precautions, sunburns can occur here year-round. Cool mountain mornings can quickly heat up. The best advice is to plan on layering your clothing. Shed a layer when you get too hot, but make sure you have an extra layer available to break a sudden chill. The layer closest to your skin should wick away sweat from your skin—lightweight wool, polyester, or polypropylene all work well (not cotton, not even for underwear). For the middle layer, choose a fabric that insulates and keeps heat in, such as polyester fleece, wool, microfiber insulation, or down. You might want to double up on the middle layer for particularly cold days. The outer layer should be material that repels wind, snow, and rain.

FLORA AND FAUNA

Wyoming is home to an impressive amount of biodiversity, and the Bighorns are no exception. From the tiniest shrew to the largest moose, the mammal life in these mountains is incredible.

Peaking in late June and early July, the wildflowers can be incredible in the Bighorns. Look for the state flower, Indian paintbrush. Balsamroot, lupine, sticky geranium, and aster are also common. Other favorites include elephant head, prairie smoke, shooting star, and fireweed. The most abundant tree in the Bighorn Mountains is the lodgepole pine. Forty percent of the trees are lodgepole. Other conifers include subalpine fir (30 percent), Engelmann spruce (14 percent), Douglas-fir (10 percent), limber pine (3 percent), and Rocky Mountain juniper (2 percent). Ponderosa pine (1 percent) can be found in drier sites at lower elevations. Pockets of the deciduous aspen (1 percent) are mixed in with the conifers. Look for their quaking leaves shimmer with a golden tinged yellow hue each fall.

Hikes might encounter mule deer, elk, or moose. Mule deer are widespread and are often seen. Moose prefer willow habitats with popular viewing locations that include the West Tensleep drainage, and the northern Bighorns along Red Grade Road. Rarely far from timber, herds of elk can sometimes be seen grazing the edges of open meadows, especially in the early morning and late evening hours. Pronghorn and white-tailed deer are found on the plains at the base of the Bighorns.

Aster
TIM FEATHERS

Although they are rarely seen, both black bears and mountain lions are found throughout the Bighorns. Coyotes are far more likely to be spotted. Coyote scat is often on the hiking trails, where the animals mark their territories.

The chatter of red squirrels is a common commotion in the forests. Look for middens, which are piles of pinecone scales that accumulate at a squirrel's favorite snacking perch. Pika are high-elevation specialists. Look for these rabbit relatives collecting grasses to store for winter in their homes among the rocky talus and boulder fields.

Birdlife in the Bighorns changes seasonally. Some species thrive here year-round. No hike or snowshoe adventure would be complete without hearing the cheery calls of black-capped and mountain chickadees. One way to separate the two bird species is to remember that mountain chickadee has snowy white stripes on the top of the head, which the black-capped chickadee lacks. Both ruffed and dusky (formerly blue) grouse are found on the Bighorns and have unique displays when trying to attract mates. Ruffed grouse appear to beat their chests with their wings, making a steady thumping sound not unlike that of a tractor starting up on a cold morning. Dusky grouse make a hollow hooting while inflating sacs along their throats. Curious by nature, another bird you might find in the Bighorns is the gray jay. Or more likely it will find you. These "camp robbers" often patrol picnic areas looking for leftovers. Do your part to keep the forest natural by always cleaning up after yourself.

Dusky Grouse
JARREN KUIPERS

The Bighorns is an island of mountain habitat. Some species, especially amphibians that lack the ability to move large distances through unsuitable habitat, are isolated from other populations because of this. Little is known about the amphibians of the Bighorns, but Colombian spotted-frog, wood frog, and northern leopard frogs all occur in limited numbers and distribution.

Reptiles live at lower elevations, including the foothills of the Bighorns. Look for eastern short-horned lizards, affectionately known as horny toads, especially in the Bighorn Basin to the west. Garter snakes are the most likely snake to be found. Bullsnakes and prairie rattlesnakes are rarely seen, but do occur in limited numbers on the prairies surrounding the Bighorns. All reptiles perform important roles in the ecosystem and should be left alone if found.

Popular game fish in the Bighorns include cutthroat, brook, brown, and rainbow trout. Golden trout are found in a few lakes. Also limited in distribution are Artic grayling, identified by an oversize dorsal fin. Anglers should consult with Wyoming Game & Fish for license and regulation requirements.

Insects can provide food for fish and birds making them an essential part of the landscape. Unfortunately, they can also make a meal out of you and me. The biting flies and mosquitoes can, at times, be locally abundant. They can also be noticeably absent. The best bet is to assume they will be an issue and be prepared. Worst-case scenario is you carried a bottle of bug spray or a long-sleeved shirt that you ended up not needing.

Hunting and fishing are popular pastimes throughout the Bighorns. Licensed hunters can target several big game and trophy species, including elk, moose, mule deer, black bear, and mountain lion. Small game includes snowshoe hare and red squirrels. Licensed anglers can expect brook, rainbow, brown, and cutthroat trout in many of the streams and lakes of the region. Golden trout and grayling are also found in a few locations. Fish stocking takes place by helicopter in some cases, and fingerling fish between 2.5 and 4 inches are released into high-elevation ponds. Only a small percentage of wilderness lakes are maintained with fish stocking efforts. Others have self-sustaining populations of fish. And the remaining waters remain fishless.

Wyoming Game & Fish Department manages hunting and fishing licensing and regulations throughout the state. For current information, contact the agency.

Wyoming Game & Fish Department
5400 Bishop Blvd.
Cheyenne, WY 82009
(307) 777-4600

SPECIAL RESTRICTIONS AND REGULATIONS

The majority of the hikes in this guide fall under the management of the Bighorn National Forest, including the hikes in the Cloud Peak Wilderness. Hiking in the wilderness requires a free permit and is subject to additional regulation. Permits can be obtained at Forest Service offices and at major trailheads throughout the forest. A few hikes are on Bureau of Land Management lands, while others cross wildlife management areas that are administered by the Wyoming Game & Fish Department. The City of Buffalo is responsible for the Clear Creek Trail in conjunction with numerous partners.

For the most current information regarding almost anything in the Bighorn Mountains, start with the Bighorn National Forest Service offices. The staff is extremely knowledgeable and friendly. In my experience, they are happy to provide information about trails, permits, regulations, and even advice on the best options for your specific interests.

A couple of special regulations are worth pointing out. These rules are essential in providing positive recreation experiences for forest users, as well as for protecting the natural resources. Seasonal regulations, such as campfire restrictions, are often implemented. Always consult with the Forest Service staff for the most current information.

Anyone entering the Cloud Peak Wilderness is required to obtain a free permit. These are available at Forest Service offices and most major trailheads, including Hunter, Circle Park, West Tensleep, Battle Park, Adelaide, Coney Creek, Coffeen Park, and at Poverty Flats. Consult the permit for additional wilderness regulations.

Far from a comprehensive list, here is a sampling of regulations:

Building, maintaining, attending, or using a campfire, other than a self-contained chemical stove above 9,200 feet in elevation is prohibited.

Below 9,200 feet in elevation, campfires must be contained on a fire blanket or within a fire pan or enclosed stove so as not to be directly on the ground.

Camping within 100 feet of all lakes, streams or other free flowing water is prohibited.

Areas of high use are subject to additional regulations in an effort to provide positive recreational experiences and protect the natural resources. Human waste and used toilet paper must be packed out and removed from National Forest System land in the West and Middle Tensleep drainages north of Tyrrell Work Center, including a portion of the Cloud Peak Wilderness.

Contact Information

United States Department of Agriculture, Forest Service
Bighorn National Forest offices are open 8:00 a.m. to 4:30 p.m. Mon through Fri, except federal holidays.

Bighorn National Forest
2013 Eastside 2nd St.
Sheridan, WY 82801
(307) 674-2600
Telephone for the Hearing Impaired
(307) 674-2604
http://www.fs.usda.gov/bighorn

Bighorn National Forest Medicine Wheel Ranger District
95 Hwy. 16/20
Greybull, WY 82426
(307) 765-4435
http://www.fs.usda.gov/bighorn

Bighorn National Forest Powder River Ranger District
1415 Fort St.
Buffalo, WY 82834
(307) 684-7806
http://www.fs.usda.gov/bighorn

Bighorn National Forest Tongue Ranger District
2013 Eastside 2nd St.
Sheridan, WY 82801
(307) 674-2600
http://www.fs.usda.gov/bighorn

Bureau of Land Management Buffalo Field Office
1425 Fort St.
Buffalo, WY 82834
(307) 684-1100
http://www.blm.gov/wy/st/en/field_offices/Buffalo.html

Bureau of Land Management Worland Field Office
101 South 23rd St.
Worland, WY 82401
(307) 347-5100
http://www.blm.gov/wy/st/en/field_offices/Worland.html

Bureau of Land Management Cody Field Office
1002 Blackburn St.
Cody, WY 82414
(307) 578-5900
http://www.blm.gov/wy/st/en/field_offices/Cody.html

City of Buffalo
46 North Main
Buffalo, WY 82834
(307) 684-5566
http://cityofbuffalowy.com/

Wyoming Game & Fish Department
5400 Bishop Blvd.
Cheyenne, WY 82009
(307) 777-4600

PLANNING YOUR TRIP

MAPS

This book is meant to be a great resource, but you should consider supplementing the material with additional maps. The Bighorn National Forest map is updated regularly, and it contains great information about campgrounds, points of interest, and current regulations. The National Geographic Cloud Peak Wilderness Map (Map 720) provides a closer look at the area of the Bighorns within the wilderness boundary. The USGS Topographical Maps are increasingly available online in addition to printed formats. The human features like trails and roads tend to be a bit dated on some of the older topo quads, but they still provide the best look at the topography and features of an area. Coupled with a bit of compass knowledge, these provide the most reliable way to navigate in the backcountry. Unlike a global positioning system (GPS), the batteries never run out on a compass. Also note that more than once, I have used a GPS to follow along a faint course only to eventually realize that the on the ground trail was a well-trodden path in the immediate vicinity.

ROAD CONDITIONS

The primitive roads of the Bighorn Mountains are notoriously gnarly. In many cases, it makes the most sense to park the rig and hike the "road" for an extra mile or two. It's important to keep in mind that a high-clearance vehicle might get you in on a road easy enough, but if one of the unpredictable pop-up thunderstorms rolls in, you are stuck. The road will be impassable at best, and at worst you'll make it back out, but you'll tear up the road and leave behind unacceptable ruts in your wake.

Especially off of US Hwy. 16, the primitive roads can be quite rocky. It is wise to check your spare tire before heading off on an adventure in the Bighorns. That said, there are decent roads to get you to plenty of trailheads, even with a low clearance vehicle. I put hundreds of miles on my first car, a 1979 Ford Fiesta, on the roads of the Bighorns.

With three scenic byways crossing the Bighorn Mountains, there are miles of highway with gorgeous views. Yet these roads can experience winter conditions any time of the year. And as the saying goes, there are two seasons in Wyoming, winter and road construction. For current conditions, contact Wyoming Road and Travel at 1-888-WYO-ROAD (1-888-996-7623) or http://wyoroad.info/.

One more thing, don't rely on online map searches for directions to trailheads. These will send you over some impassable roads, especially on Bureau of Land Management lands on the western side of the Bighorns.

WATER

Even in frigid conditions, you need at least two quarts of water a day to function efficiently. Add heat and taxing terrain and you can bump that figure up to one gallon. That's simply a base to work from—your metabolism and your level of conditioning can raise or lower that amount. Unless you know your level, assume that you need one gallon of water a day. Now, where do you plan on getting the water? Preferably not from natural water sources. These sources can be loaded with intestinal disturbers, such as bacteria, viruses, and fertilizers. *Giardia lamblia,* the most common of these disturbers, is a protozoan parasite that lives part of its life cycle as a cyst in water sources. The parasite spreads when mammals defecate in water sources. Once ingested, *Giardia* can induce cramping, diarrhea, vomiting, and fatigue within two days to two weeks after ingestion. Giardiasis is treatable with prescription drugs. If you believe you've contracted giardiasis, see a doctor immediately.

TREATING WATER

The best and easiest solution to avoid polluted water is to carry your water with you. Yet, depending on the nature of your hike and the duration, this may not be an option—one gallon of water weighs 8.5 pounds. In that case, you'll need to look into treating water. Regardless of which method you choose, you should always carry some water with you in case of an emergency. Save this reserve until you absolutely need it.

There are three methods of treating water: boiling, chemical treatment, and filtering. If you boil water, it's recommended that you do so for 10–15 minutes. This is often impractical because you're forced to exhaust a great deal of your fuel supply. You can opt for chemical treatment, which will kill *Giardia* but will not take care of other chemical pollutants. Another drawback to chemical treatments is the unpleasant taste of the water after it's treated. You can remedy this by adding powdered drink mix to the water. Filters are the preferred method for treating water. Many filters remove *Giardia,* organic and inorganic contaminants, and don't leave an aftertaste. However, water filters are far from perfect as they can easily become clogged or leak if a gasket wears out. It's always a good idea to carry a backup supply of chemical treatment tablets in case your filter decides to quit on you.

It's important to always carry plenty of water and to stop often and drink fluids regularly, even if you aren't thirsty.

DEHYDRATION

Hiking at altitudes in the Bighorns means you'll need more water than the average person, who requires about 2 quarts per day. Exactly how much you need depends on the climate and your level of exertion. When hiking in hot weather, you'll be sweating heavily. Not only will you need more water to replace fluid loss, you'll need electrolytes, too. Munching on salty trail mix or sipping diluted sports drinks will help replenish your body. In cold weather, it's equally important to drink extra water since cold, dry air can remove water from your skin quicker than when it is hot and humid. Aim to drink about a quart per hour of intense hiking and know the signs of dehydration, which include: headache, thirst, less frequent urination, dark-colored urine, weakness, and dizziness.

If you become dehydrated, take a break and begin drinking small amounts of water over a period of time. Don't be tempted to chug a huge amount, or you might throw up, further exasperating the problem.

The best advice I can give about hydration is to begin hiking fully hydrated. Start drinking water about 3–4 hours before you hit the trail and maintain your fluid status with plenty of water breaks.

ALTITUDE SICKNESS

Even if you are in great shape, you may be at risk for altitude sickness, also known as acute mountain sickness. This condition can happen to hikers upon reaching high altitudes, generally around 8,000 feet above sea level and higher. Because the air pressure is thinner at these heights, hikers are prone to mild or more severe side effects as a result of lower oxygen levels.

The highest point in the Bighorns is Cloud Peak at 13,166 feet. While many of the hikes in this guide are less than 10,000 feet in elevation, most hikes are pushing 8,000+ feet, so it is important to recognize the signs of altitude sickness and understand basic prevention strategies. Symptoms include headache, loss of appetite, fatigue, not sleeping well, and feeling dizzy. But don't be fooled if you feel fine the first day of hiking. Many times symptoms do not occur until the second day. More severe symptoms occur when the condition begins to affect your brain or lungs. These include confusion, not being able to walk straight, blue lips, feeling faint, shortness of breath, and chest tightness. Keep an eye on others in your group and take action if you notice any of the above symptoms.

The best treatment for altitude sickness is to safely proceed to lower elevation. People with more severe mountain sickness may need to go to the hospital for oxygen and medication. To help prevent this condition from happening, plan to ascend gradually with plenty of breaks; avoid alcohol; stay hydrated; and eat regular high-energy meals.

Even if you are living in Wyoming, don't rule out the effects high mountain elevation can have on you. I've hiked with people who have spent their whole lives in Wyoming, and they experienced minor altitude sickness when climbing Cloud Peak. I've also hiked with friends from outside the area, who felt the symptoms of altitude sickness at much lower elevations.

WATER CROSSINGS

In the Bighorns, there are plenty of times when you can navigate water crossings without actually having to get wet. You can occasionally step over the trickle of water. Or there is a conveniently located downed log allowing you to showcase your gymnastic talents on the balance beam, while maintaining dry feet. In other instances, a wet crossing is unavoidable. With the exception to spring runoff season when the water can be raging, most crossings in the Bighorns are very manageable. That said, drowning and hypothermia are always a legitimate concern, and every water crossing should be taken seriously.

I always carry a pair of strap-on sandals (not flip-flops) for such crossings. I hate crossing barefooted. I always seem to find a rouge stick to stab myself with, or I stub a toe on a rock. To me there is no sense in hiking in wet shoes either. I also carry extra socks, but it could be argued that I'm a bit overprotective of my feet. No matter your chosen footwear, here are a couple of pointers for crossing moving water:

Unbuckle Your Pack

Unbuckling your hip and chest straps on your backpack will make it easier to take off if you happen to have a misstep and take a plunge. The weight of the pack can keep you down, and it's far better to retrieve your pack downstream than to be fighting it in the moment.

Face Upstream

The natural tendency is to face the opposite shore and walk directly toward it. When you're walking in flowing water though, the current will be pushing you off balance. It's far better to face upstream, keeping your knees slightly bent, and shuffling side to side when crossing. Don't cross your feet either. Instead, focus on your footing and navigate little by little.

Find a Good Foothold

Wet round river rocks aren't ideal for traction. Make sure you have a secure footing before shifting your weight and moving your body. You might have to navigate around a few boulders to get to the other side. You're looking for the path of least resistance, not the straightest shot to the other side.

Use Walking Sticks

You might not need them for smaller or slower moving water, but for swift currents and deeper waters, by all means, use a walking stick or two to help you maintain your balance. They don't even have to be fancy ski poles or walking sticks that you carry with you. Just find a downed tree branch to use if need be.

Practice

Stream crossings are one of the most unnatural aspects of hiking. If you are inexperienced with the techniques, give it a bit of practice, and work your way up to major crossings.

HYPOTHERMIA

Even during mild-weather days, you can get hypothermia, especially if it's windy or wet. Hypothermia is when your body loses heat faster than it can produce it, leading to a dangerously low body temperature. Warning signs include uncontrolled shivering, slurred speech, fatigue, confusion, and clumsy movements.

To prevent hypothermia, dress in layers. Make sure the layer closest to your skin wicks away sweat from your skin—lightweight wool, polyester, or polypropylene all work well (not cotton, not even for underwear). For the middle layer, choose a fabric that insulates and keeps heat in, such as polyester fleece, wool, microfiber insulation, or down. You might want to double up on the middle layer for particularly cold days. The outer layer should be material that repels wind, snow, and rain. Protect your head, hands, and feet with a warm hat, mittens (which are warmer than gloves), wool socks, and waterproof boots. Also key to preventing hypothermia is adequate nutrition. Drink plenty of fluids and fuel up with carbohydrate-rich foods. Your body requires energy to stay warm.

If you need to treat someone with hypothermia, start by adding layers of dry clothing, increasing physical activity and seeking warm shelter. If no shelter is around, add heat with warm water bottles or a heat compress around the neck, armpits, and groin, and build a campfire if possible. Also make sure the person is drinking fluids—warm sugar water is ideal—and consuming high-energy foods such as carbohydrate-rich trail mix. Body-to-body contact will also help transfer heat. That might mean getting into a sleeping bag wearing dry lightweight clothing with the hypothermic person also in dry lightweight clothing.

LEAVE NO TRACE

Coupled with the planning ahead and preparedness are the Leave No Trace Seven Principles established by the Leave No Trace Center for Outdoor Ethics. These easy-to-follow procedures help hikers, campers, and everyone who enjoys nature to respectfully care for public lands. The USDA Forest Service encourages all visitors to the Bighorn Mountains to practice these eco-friendly guidelines during your outdoor adventures. The following principles are © 1999 by the Leave No Trace Center for Outdoor Ethics: www.LNT.org.

LEAVE NO TRACE SEVEN PRINCIPLES

Plan Ahead and Prepare
- Know the regulations and special concerns for the area you'll visit.
- Prepare for extreme weather, hazards, and emergencies.
- Schedule your trip to avoid times of high use.
- Visit in small groups when possible. Consider splitting larger groups into smaller groups.
- Repackage food to minimize waste.
- Use a map and compass to eliminate the use of marking paint, rock cairns, or flagging.

Travel and Camp on Durable Surfaces
- Durable surfaces include established trails and campsites, rock, gravel, dry grasses, or snow.
- Protect riparian areas by camping at least 200 feet from lakes and streams.
- Good campsites are found, not made. Altering a site is not necessary.

In popular areas
- Concentrate use on existing trails and campsites.
- Walk single file in the middle of the trail, even when wet or muddy.
- Keep campsites small. Focus activity in areas where vegetation is absent.

In pristine areas
- Disperse use to prevent the creation of campsites and trails.
- Avoid places where impacts are just beginning.

Dispose of Waste Properly
- Pack it in, pack it out. Inspect your campsite and rest areas for trash or spilled foods. Pack out all trash, leftover food, and litter.
- Deposit solid human waste in catholes dug 6–8 inches deep, at least 200 feet from water, camp, and trails. Cover and disguise the cathole when finished.
- Pack out toilet paper and hygiene products.
- To wash yourself or your dishes, carry water 200 feet away from streams or lakes and use small amounts of biodegradable soap. Scatter strained dishwater.

Leave What You Find
- Preserve the past: Examine, but do not touch cultural or historic structures and artifacts.
- Leave rocks, plants, and other natural objects as you find them.
- Avoid introducing or transporting nonnative species.
- Do not build structures, furniture, or dig trenches.

Minimize Campfire Impacts

- Campfires can cause lasting impacts to the backcountry. Use a lightweight stove for cooking and enjoy a candle lantern for light.
- Where fires are permitted, use established fire rings, fire pans, or mound fires.
- Keep fires small. Only use sticks from the ground that can be broken by hand.
- Burn all wood and coals to ash, put out campfires completely, then scatter cool ashes.

Respect Wildlife

- Observe wildlife from a distance. Do not follow or approach them.
- Never feed animals. Feeding wildlife damages their health, alters natural behaviors, and exposes them to predators and other dangers.
- Protect wildlife and your food by storing rations and trash securely.
- Control pets at all times, or leave them at home.
- Avoid wildlife during sensitive times: mating, nesting, raising young, or winter.

Be Considerate of Other Visitors

- Respect other visitors and protect the quality of their experience.
- Be courteous. Yield to other users on the trail.
- Step to the downhill side of the trail when encountering pack stock.
- Take breaks and camp away from trails and other visitors.
- Let nature's sounds prevail. Avoid loud voices and noises.

Hazelton Peak
LINDA LULIAS

BUFFALO AND SOUTHEAST WILDERNESS ACCESS

The Cloud Peak Skyway Scenic Byway (US Hwy. 16) runs from Buffalo, over Powder River Pass, and down to Ten Sleep, and is the artery for hikes in this region.

Grouse Mountain, Mosier Gulch, and the Clear Creek Trail System connect the quaint community of Buffalo to the Bighorn National Forest.

The Clear Creek Watershed dominates the stretch of mountains from Buffalo to Powder River Pass. Here on the eastern slopes of the Bighorns, the granite peaks are accessible via timbered climbs. Fishable lakes including those of the Circle Park Loop, Long and Ringbone Lakes, and Lake Angeline make ideal destinations of varying distances.

The Hunter Corrals Trailhead provides a rare access road that is suitable for all vehicles. From here, hikers have the flexibility of day trips to multiday backpacking adventures encompassing the entire Cloud Peak Wilderness via the Solitude Loop Trail including Florence Pass which provides one of just three footpaths crossing the divide of the Bighorns.

The peaks of the Bighorn
Mountains from Cull Watt Park
LINDA LULIAS

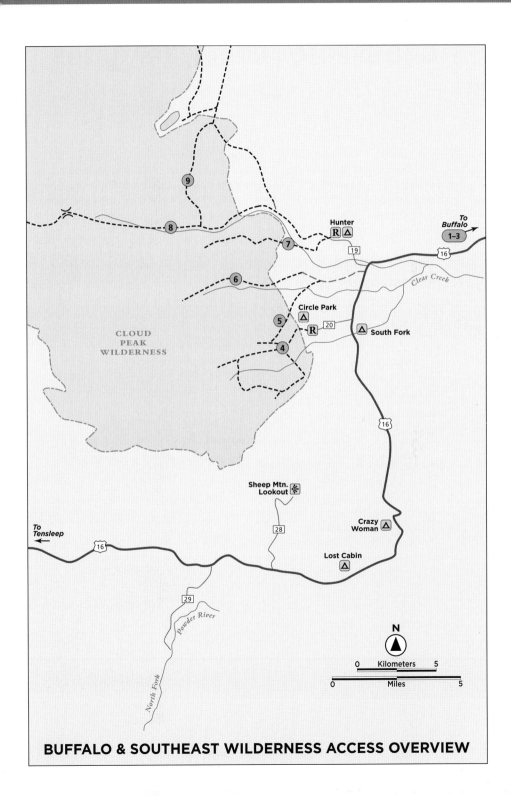

BUFFALO & SOUTHEAST WILDERNESS ACCESS OVERVIEW

1. GROUSE MOUNTAIN, TRAIL 205

WHY GO?

Constructed in 2011, Grouse Mountain is one of the newest trails in the Bighorn National Forest. It can be a nice early-season walk while much of the high country is still under a blanket of snow. Early summer wildflowers can be impressive on the upper stretches. Expect to share the trail with cows and mountain bikers later in the season.

THE RUNDOWN

Distance: 2.2 miles one-way point-to-point or 4.4 miles out-and-back

Elevation gain: 1,055 feet

Difficulty: Moderate due to steep terrain, uneven footing, and elevation gains

Hiking time: About 3 hours

Best seasons: Spring, fall

Fees and permits: No fees or permits required

Trail contacts: Bighorn National Forest, 2013 Eastside 2nd St., Sheridan, WY 82801, (307) 674-2600, http://www.fs.usda.gov/bighorn

Maps: USDA Forest Service Bighorn National Forest, USGS North Ridge

Dog-friendly: Dogs must be under control

Trail surface: Uneven terrain

Nearest town: Buffalo, Wyoming

Other trail users: Mountain bikers

FINDING THE TRAILHEAD

From US Hwy. 16, the well-marked exit turns south for Grouse Mountain Trailhead (FR 402). This road goes east about a mile, through a gate (if you found it closed, close it behind you). Don't be confused by the private inholding signage. Beyond the gate, the road turns to FR 403. You'll initially notice Trail 217 that heads south into the Brush Creek drainage. The Grouse Mountain Trailhead is about three quarters of a mile farther. **Trailhead GPS:** N44 19.254' / W106 51.079'

THE HIKE

The Grouse Mountain Trail (Trail 205) is one of the first trails you reach on the Bighorn National Forest when you leave Buffalo. If you plan a shuttle, you can even hike all of the way back to Buffalo when you couple Grouse Mountain with Mosier Gulch (Hike 2) and the Clear Creek Trail (Hike 3). An epic and mostly downhill hike would start at Grouse Mountain and end at the Dash Inn Restaurant in Buffalo. If you are hiking this trail as an out-and-back, I'd suggest starting at Mosier Gulch and hiking uphill first.

Be sure to look west at the mountains before heading east down Trail 205. You'll quickly lose sight of them as you head over the crest of the hill, but fear not, the wide-open vistas to the east are equally as breathtaking. The trail heads downhill, from the parking area, weaving in wide meandering switchbacks along a pasture of grasses and forbs.

The forested slopes of Grouse Mountain serve as a visual contrast to the open prairies ahead. Here is a nice example of aspect, with the cooler and wetter north facing slopes forested, while the drier southern faces grow grasses and rock outcroppings.

Cattle graze this stretch of trail, but they seem content to watch you stroll by. This is a mixed-use trail and is increasingly popular with mountain bikers and horseback riders. It amuses me to think about how cows ponder bicyclists.

You'll step over a couple of minor water crossing about a mile into the hike. Here the cows will begrudgingly give up their corner of shade as you pass by. Tucked in a little grove of aspens, the Bighorn National Forest boundary is marked with a closed gate about mile from the trailhead.

Ruffed Grouse on
Grouse Mountain Trail

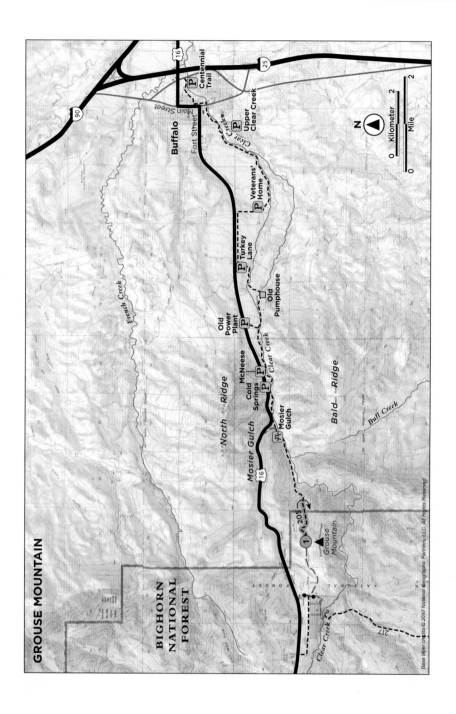

GROUSE MOUNTAIN

BIGHORN NATIONAL FOREST

Buffalo

Main Street

Fort Street

Centennial Trail

Upper Clear Creek

Clear Creek

Veterans' Home

Turkey Lane

Old Pumphouse

Old Power Plant

McNeese

Cold Springs

Clear Creek

Mosier Gulch

North Ridge

Mosier Gulch

Bald Ridge

Bull Creek

French Creek

Grouse Mountain

Clear Creek

N

0 Kilometer 2

0 Mile 2

Peaks from Grouse Mountain Trail

The final mile stretch is marked by an increase in tree cover and an increase in switchbacks as you continue to drop elevation with every step. Clear Creek approaches from the south as Grouse Mountain and Mosier Gulch trails come together.

I was fortunate enough to encounter a ruffed grouse when I hiked Grouse Mountain, although I can't make any promises for your visit. You might also encounter dusky grouse (formerly known as blue grouse) and mule deer.

MILES AND DIRECTIONS

0.0   Trail departs from FR 403.

1.2   Bighorn National Forest boundary.

2.2   Trail meets western end of Mosier Gulch Trail (Hike 2).

2. MOSIER GULCH

WHY GO?

Mosier Gulch picnic area is a lovely stop tucked into the ponderosa forests just west of Buffalo. Hikers can make a day of it exploring along Clear Creek. Mosier Gulch connects to the Grouse Mountain Trail (Hike 1) to the west and the Clear Creek Trail (Hike 3) to the east.

THE RUNDOWN

Distance: 1.2 miles connecting trail or 2.4 miles out-and-back

Elevation gain: 170 feet

Difficulty: Easy due to mostly level terrain along a roadbed

Hiking time: About 1 hour

Best seasons: Spring, summer, fall

Fees and permits: No fees or permits required

Trail contacts: Bureau of Land Management Buffalo Field Office, 1425 Fort St., Buffalo, WY 82834, (307) 684-1100, http://www.blm.gov/wy/st/en/ field_offices/Buffalo.html; City of Buffalo, 46 North Main, Buffalo, WY 82834, (307) 684-5566, http://cityofbuffalowy.com/

Maps: USDA Forest Service Bighorn National Forest, USGS North Ridge

Dog-friendly: Dogs must be under control

Trail surface: Gravel road

Nearest town: Buffalo, Wyoming

Other trail users: Mountain bikers, joggers

FINDING THE TRAILHEAD

 Take US Hwy. 16 west from Buffalo for about 5 miles. The Mosier Gulch Picnic Area is well marked with signs. Parking is available near the picnic area above, but hikers can also park in pullouts below.

Trailhead GPS: N44 19.816' / W106 48.794'

THE HIKE

Mosier Gulch is an under-appreciated gem. The picnic area offers up picnic tables, pedestal fire grates, and a toilet. Clear Creek flows along the trail, and fishing is allowed on the adjacent City of Buffalo property. Hikers and mountain bikers can use this spot as pickup and save themselves going back up the Grouse Mountain Trail.

The trailhead near the picnic area provides good access to the William J. Mentock section of the Clear Creek Trail (Hike 3). Hikers headed west can use pull-outs at the bottom of the hill for parking. Broad-tailed hummingbirds may greet you at the parking lot.

The Mosier Gulch trail begins at a closed gate on the western end of the lower parking area. Bald Ridge stands tall like a beacon on the opposite side of the creek. The walking is easy over this gravel road. Listen to the sounds of Clear Creek churning past as it gains momentum flowing down from the mountain.

Chokecherry brambles spring up alongside the trail. The occasional aspen tree is also present with its leaves a quaking. Ponderosa pine also stand tall, identified by their long needles. Find one and give it a big sniff along its thick reddish bark. What does it smell like to you? Butterscotch? Vanilla?

On the western edge of the hike, about 1.2 miles from the parking lot, a small dam pools up Clear Creek. Not far from here, you'll see the signs marking the Grouse Mountain Trail (Trail 205, Hike 1). Ambitious hikers can head up the switchbacks as far as they'd like. Others will turn back here, retracing their steps to the parking lot.

The Mosier Gulch Picnic Area was established in 1986 on lands that were originally the Fort McKinney Military Reserve dating back to 1879. A trail originally used by Native Americans later became a wagon road up the mountain that was used by the army. In 1912, the first automobile traveled the route, which was eventually known as the Black and Yellow Trail. By 1926, the route was designated as State Hwy. 16.

Bald Ridge from Mosier Gulch Trail

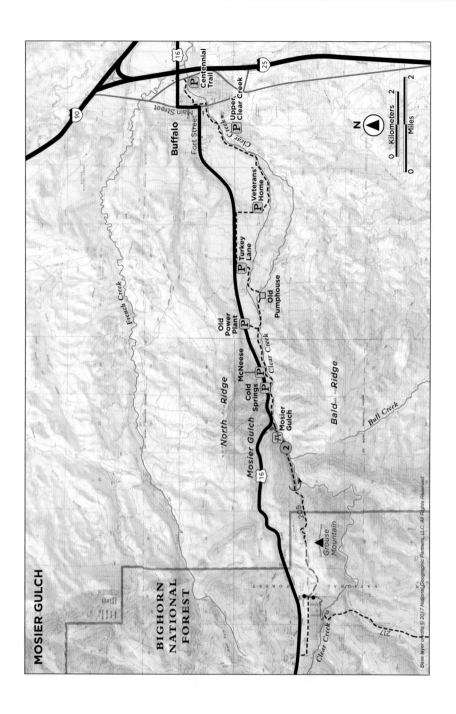

MOSIER GULCH

BIGHORN NATIONAL FOREST

Buffalo

Main Street

Fort Street

16

90

25

P Centennial Trail

P Upper Clear Creek

Clear Creek

P Veterans' Home

P Turkey Lane

Old Pumphouse

P Old Power Plant

Clear Creek

McNeese

P P Cold Springs

Mosier Gulch

North Ridge

French Creek

Bald Ridge

Bull Creek

2 Mosier Gulch

16

205

Grouse Mountain

NATIONAL FOREST

Clear Creek

217

N

0 Kilometers 2

0 Miles 2

Chokecherries

MILES AND DIRECTIONS

0.0 Trail leaves Mosier Gulch Picnic Area lower parking lot.

1.2 Trail connects with Grouse Mountain Trail (Hike 1).

3. CLEAR CREEK TRAIL

WHY GO?

This trail is a true testament to the community nature of Buffalo, Wyoming. It has been pieced together over the years and was in collaboration between numerous agencies, landowners, and volunteers. Improvements and access points are added each season. With multiple access points, you can take a short stroll or be out all day. The views of the Bighorns are stunning, and much of the trail is within earshot of Clear Creek.

THE RUNDOWN

Distance: 9.2 miles point-to-point, many shorter segments as out-and-backs

Elevation gain: 1,000 feet

Difficulty: Easy in eastern sections due to mostly level terrain, moderate in western section due to uneven footing and elevation gains

Hiking time: Varies

Best seasons: Year-round

Fees and permits: No fees or permits required

Trail contacts: City of Buffalo/ Buffalo Trails Board, 46 North Main, Buffalo, WY 82834,

(307) 684-5566, http://cityof buffalowy.com/

Maps: Clear Creek Trail Map, USGS North Ridge

Dog-friendly: Leashed dogs permitted on most sections; no dogs allowed on Veterans' Home sections

Trail surface: Mostly smooth path with some pavement, gravel road, and sidewalk, but westernmost segment is uneven terrain

Nearest town: Buffalo, Wyoming

Other trail users: Bicyclers, joggers, and dog walkers

FINDING THE TRAILHEAD

Take US Hwy. 16 west from Buffalo for about 5 miles. The Mosier Gulch Picnic Area is well marked with signs. Parking is available near the picnic area above, but hikers can also park in pullouts below. Additional access to the Clear Creek Trail is off US 16 and throughout Buffalo.

Trailhead GPS: N44 19.816' / W106 48.794' western trailhead,
N44 21.160' / W106 41.365' eastern trailhead

THE HIKE

The Clear Creek Trail has been one of the most exciting additions to the Buffalo area. It took years of coordinated efforts, between multiple agencies and

Clear Creek Trail's namesake body of water

The foothills and peaks rise from the Clear Creek Trail near Buffalo

landowners to come to fruition. The lower stretches near town are most popular with local walkers, but the entire stretch from Mosier Gulch to the Centennial Trail on the east end is quite lovely.

The William J. Mentock segment of the Clear Creek trail is the westernmost stretch. Bill Mentock was the national recipient of the Take Pride in America Awards Program for his work on the Clear Creek Trail System, and this stretch is named in his honor. From the Mosier Gulch Picnic Area, head over the sturdy bridge and down the trail. Another option is to park below the picnic area at the base of the hill. You can head east from there, and you'll quickly meet up with the upper trail descending from the picnic area. The merged trail continues east along Clear Creek. Ponderosa pine trees and Clear Creek rumbling down its boulder-filled streambed characterize this stretch of trail. You'll find spur trails leading to parking areas along US Hwy. 16 as you go, with Cold Springs Access 0.9 mile from Mosier Gulch and McNeese Access 1.3 miles from the parking lot.

A few small footbridges lead you over wet areas of the trail. Ample benches offer up resting points along the way. Both mule deer and white-tailed deer can be spotted along the Clear Creek Trail. The birding is excellent here, too, especially during spring and fall migration.

One and a quarter miles or so beyond the McNeese Access hikers will come to the Old Pumphouse. This is also accessible directly from US Hwy. 16 as a short lollipop hike. The pumphouse has unfortunately been the target of excess graffiti and detracts from the natural scenery of Clear Creek.

Clear Creek

Beyond the pumphouse is the Grouse Mountain Archery Association Range, although the main trail skirts around it. Hikers should also be aware that sections of the Clear Creek Trail are open to archery hunting and fishing during certain seasons. Be sure to check with local authorities for the latest regulations.

The Mentock leg of the trail ends at the parking lot off of Turkey Lane, just shy of 4 miles from Mosier Gulch. Hikers can continue on, walking north for a quarter of a mile to the Highway 16 Bike Path. As it marches alongside the highway, this one-mile stretch is the least appealing segment of the Clear Creek Trail. It does, however, bring back fond memories for me. Growing up I wore a rut into this path putting in countless miles on my bike here.

The bike path and the highway continue east down the hill to Buffalo, but hikers should hang a right and head south along Veterans' Lane. This tree-lined driveway goes to the Fort McKinney Veterans' Home of Wyoming. It also leads to the trailhead through Veterans' Home Pasture. Dogs are not allowed on this section of trail. The Clear Creek Trail takes on more of a high plains feel as it crosses sagebrush flats here. You skirt the riparian corridor of cottonwoods as you hike eastward. This 1.1-mile stretch offers neat looks at both the Bighorn Mountains and the town of Buffalo.

A short spur to the south leads to the parking area off of Upper Clear Creek Road. It is worth the few paces to see the historic 1880 steel Pony Truss Bridge. This bridge is uniquely designed and likely functioned as a railroad bridge originally.

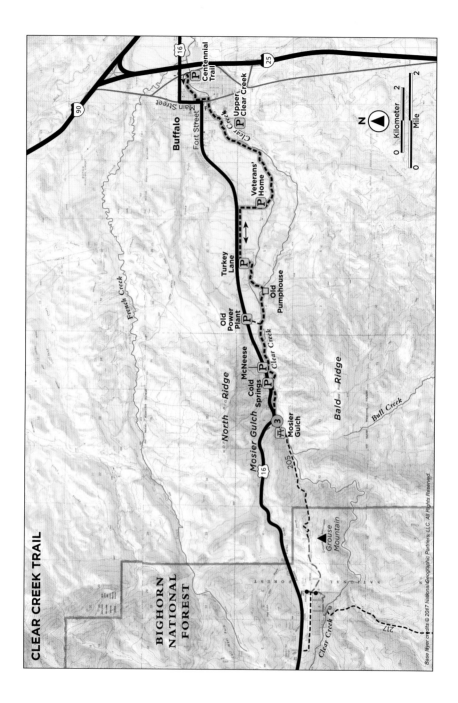

CLEAR CREEK TRAIL

BIGHORN NATIONAL FOREST

Buffalo

Centennial Trail

Upper Clear Creek

Veterans' Home

Turkey Lane

Old Pumphouse

Old Power Plant

McNeese

Cold Springs

Mosier Gulch

Clear Creek

North Ridge

French Creek

Bald Ridge

Bull Creek

Grouse Mountain

Fort Street

Main Street

The main trail enters the Greenbelt Park at this intersection. From here, it's 1.2 miles to Klondike Road, where walkers can take the south bank of the creek through the city parks and into downtown. The Clear Creek Brewing Company and the Sports Lure are just south (to the right) on Main Street, while the trail continues north (left) on Main for two tenths of a mile to reach Trail Drive. Turn right (east) and pick up the final leg of the Clear Creek Trail, the Centennial Trail.

Here the easternmost stretch of trail offers pleasant walking along the banks of Clear Creek. Numerous interpretive display signs also highlight the history of the Buffalo region along the Centennial Trail segment.

The Clear Creek Trail reaches its eastern terminus at the Bypass Road, just south of the Dash Inn, home to the best burgers around. I recommend the Dash Burger with everything on it, a side of potato wedges with cheese and bacon, and a chocolate shake.

MILES AND DIRECTIONS

0.0   Trail leaves Mosier Gulch Picnic Area.

0.9   Spur trail to Cold Springs Access on US Hwy. 16.

1.3   Spur trail to McNeese Access on US Hwy. 16.

2.5   Old Pumphouse.

3.9   Arrive at Turkey Lane Parking.

4.2   Highway 16 Bike Path.

5.2   Turn right onto Veterans' Lane.

5.5   Veterans' Lane Trailhead.

6.6   Spur to right for 1880 bridge and Upper Clear Creek Road Trailhead.

7.8   Klondike Road.

8.3   Main Street.

8.5   Turn right onto Trail Drive.

8.6   Continue along Centennial Trail segment of Clear Creek Trail.

9.2   Arrive at eastern end of Clear Creek Trail at Bypass Road.

4. CIRCLE PARK LOOP, TRAILS 046 & 095

WHY GO?

The Circle Park Trailhead is one of the most popular, and rightfully so. It offers some of the easiest access to Cloud Peak Wilderness. This lollipop loop offers flexibility from easy day hiking to multiple night excursions. Numerous fishing lakes mean you have plenty of choices.

THE RUNDOWN

Distance: 9.4 miles overall, lollipop

Elevation gain: 1,680 feet

Difficulty: Moderate due to overall distance, uneven footing, and moderate elevation gain

Hiking time: About 6.5 hours

Best seasons: Late spring, summer, early fall

Fees and permits: Free Cloud Peak Wilderness Use Registration

Trail contacts: Bighorn National Forest, 2013 Eastside 2nd St., Sheridan, WY 82801, (307) 674-2600, http://www.fs.usda.gov/bighorn

Maps: USDA Forest Service Bighorn National Forest, National Geographic Trails Unlimited 720 Cloud Peak Wilderness, USGS Hunter Mesa, USGS Lake Angeline

Dog-friendly: Dogs must be under control

Trail surface: Uneven terrain

Nearest town: Buffalo, Wyoming

Other trail users: Equestrians

FINDING THE TRAILHEAD

 From Powder River Ranger District Office, head west on US Hwy. 16 for about 15 miles to the well-marked Circle Park Road (FR 20). Follow this for 2 miles. Bear left toward Circle Park Trailhead (FR 384), not toward the campground. The trailhead is 0.5 mile ahead.

Trailhead GPS: N44 16.594' / W106 59.096'

THE HIKE

Don't let the amount of vehicles in the parking lot concern you. Even on the most popular trails of the Bighorns, like this one, the crowds aren't overwhelming. Be sure to self-register your hiking party at the trailhead.

Take the views in along the early clearings, because much of this hike is cloaked in a canopy of trees. Lodgepole pines grow straight and tall. The walking is broken up with dog-hair stands of trees growing in as dead lodgepole snags stand tall like sentinels reminding hikers of fires from years gone by. This hike has just enough downhill segments that your mind forgets how much elevation you gain in the first two miles to Sherd Lake. Feeling completely out of place, one short section of trail has been built up and sanded in. Most of the trail is well worn, but littered with rocks to keep you focused on your next step.

The Cloud Peak Wilderness boundary is 0.6 mile up the trail. A quarter of a mile past this is a retired route that formerly connected the Circle Park Campground with the trail. Keep left to stay on the main trail, which is nearly impossible to miss.

After you climb the final pitch to Sherd Lake, the dominating view of Darton Peak makes it seem like you should be farther away from the parking lot than just 1.7 miles. Sherd Lake proper marks the beginning and ending point of the 6-mile loop.

Hang a left to head south as you follow the eastern shore of Sherd Lake. Most of the hike is trail 046, but this segment is trail 095. The trail passes numerous wooded ponds as it continues up and down a number of ridges. It ultimately bottoms out at the Duck Creek crossing, 1.2 miles from Sherd Lake. The trail winds back to the west, gaining elevation as each step brings you closer and closer to the mountain peaks, including Bighorn Peak and Loaf Mountain.

Another 0.7 mile of mostly climbing up brings you to the intersection with the trail to FR 382. Bear right to stay on the loop trail (once again trail 046 now) as it crosses boggy meadows. You'll cross Duck Creek again 0.3 mile up the trail, and a short distance beyond that, the side trail to Trigger Lake (Trail 099) materializes on the left. Trigger Lake is a popular fishing spot.

Keeping right, the loop trail pushes onward. Another mile up the trail, you'll cross South Clear Creek as it flows out of the pond known as Her Lake. A third of a mile past this, you'll find the spur trail to Old Crow Lake (Trail 090). The hike to Old Crow offers another gorgeous view of the alpine peaks to the west.

From the Old Crow junction, the loop trail generally heads in a northerly direction. It descends at first, then climbs up. Fires have always been part of the forested landscape. Here we see stands of trees that grew up following the 1943 Duck Creek Burn. This is a nice visual comparison to the 1988 Lost Fire seen throughout much of the rest of the drainage.

Otter Lake is the next body of water, 0.7 mile beyond the junction to Old Crow Lake, and 0.3 mile more brings you to the highest point along the loop trail, Rainy Lake, sitting at 9,400 feet. From here, a mile-long side trail (Trail 087), including a stretch of boulder hopping, climbs northwest up and over the ridgeline and down into Willow Lake. The main loop trail heads east and traverses the timbered ridge until dropping back down to Sherd Lake.

Near the outlet of Sherd Lake, there is a trail that heads north (left) to Schoolhouse Park Road (Trail 047, Hike 5). Instead, turn right to cross the small outlet stream, and then retrace your steps 1.7 miles back to the Circle Park Trailhead.

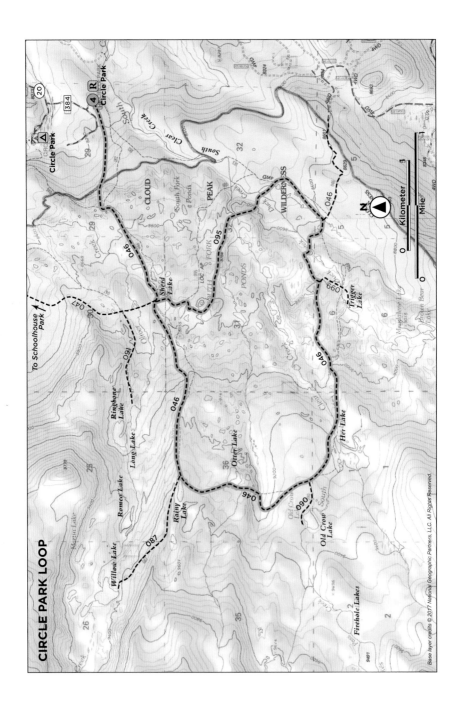

CIRCLE PARK LOOP

Sherd Lake

MILES AND DIRECTIONS

0.0 Circle Park Trailhead.

0.6 Enter Cloud Peak Wilderness.

0.8 Retired spur trail, keep left to stay on Trail 046.

1.7 Arrive at Sherd Lake. Continue left, now on Trail 095.

2.9 Duck Creek.

3.6 Continue to the right onto Trail 046.

3.9 Cross Duck Creek.

4.0 Spur Trail 099 to Trigger Lake.

5.0 Her Lake.

5.3 Spur Trail 090 to Old Crow Lake.

6.0 Otter Lake.

6.3 Rainy Lake and spur Trail 087 to Willow Lake.

7.7 Sherd Lake.

9.4 Return to Circle Park Trailhead.

5. LONG LAKE, TRAILS 047 & 091

WHY GO?

Most approach this hike from the Circle Park Trailhead and Sherd Lake, but this route is a less crowded option. The hike offers a visual reminder of the regrowth after a fire, in this case the Lost Fire of 1988.

THE RUNDOWN

Distance: 6 miles out-and-back

Elevation gain: 1,005 feet

Difficulty: Moderate due to midrange distance, moderate elevation gain

Hiking time: About 3.5 hours

Best seasons: Late spring, summer, early fall

Fees and permits: Free Cloud Peak Wilderness Use Registration

Trail contacts: Bighorn National Forest, 2013 Eastside 2nd St., Sheridan, WY 82801, (307) 674-2600, http://www.fs.usda .gov/bighorn

Maps: USDA Forest Service Bighorn National Forest, National Geographic Trails Unlimited 720 Cloud Peak Wilderness, USGS Hunter Mesa, USGS Lake Angeline

Dog-friendly: Dogs must be under control

Trail surface: Uneven terrain

Nearest town: Buffalo, Wyoming

Other trail users: Equestrians

Special considerations: There is no trail registration box at the trailhead; therefore, you'll have to obtain the free permit elsewhere, either at the Forest Service office in Buffalo or at a nearby trailhead like Hunter or Circle Park.

FINDING THE TRAILHEAD

From Buffalo head west on US Hwy. 16. Take the exit for Schoolhouse Park/Hunter Corrals. Follow the lesser road (FR 391). After 2.7 miles, turn left onto FR 387 and then left again onto FR 386. Park at the end of FR 386. Wade the creek to reach the trailhead.
Trailhead GPS: N44 18.153' / W106 59.572'

THE HIKE

For folks that remember the Lost Fire of 1988, this trail hikes into the heart of the burned area. Now some 30 years removed from the blaze, the trees are growing straight and tall. Lodgepole pine is dependent on fire, and this area continues to be a healthy and productive ecosystem. Elk especially benefit from the cover lodgepole pine stands provide.

The rough access road from Schoolhouse Park limits the amount of traffic this trail (Trail 047) receives. Most people heading to Long and Ringbone Lakes walk in from the Circle Park Loop Trail (Hike 4). Instead, this hike starts at the end of FR 386. The trail makes a shallow crossing of Middle Clear Creek. The trail continues south as it makes a steady climb up in elevation.

About halfway into the hike (around 1.5 miles), the trail enters the marshy basin valley of Sawmill Creek. The historic sawmill structure was torched in the 1988 burn. Sawmills cut tie-hacks and sent them downstream to meet demand for military forts, early settlers, and the growing railroad industry of the 1800s and early 1900s.

The lightly used trail can be a bit difficult to follow through the heart of the wet meadow as it rock-hops across Sawmill Creek. The trail continues to climb as it travels past living pines and dead snags standing tall. With breaks in the canopy, you'll see the rounded peaks of the Bighorn Mountains, with Ant Hill standing apart.

Long Lake

In a stand of trees, the trail reaches a marked intersection. Trail 047 continues on eventually connecting with the Circle Park Loop at Sherd Lake. A right turn puts you onto Trail 091 and leads west to Long and Ringbone Lakes. Oliver Creek parallels south of the trail for this stretch, although it is tucked back away from the trail a fair distance.

The landscape becomes noticeably rockier as it closes in on the high-elevation lakes situated at the base of Bighorn and Darton Peaks. The trail ends on a high point looking down on Long Lake. Anglers can toss a line, the outlet of Long Lake can be especially productive. A short but steep rock-hop crosses the divide between Long and Ringbone Lakes. There is a prolific patch of raspberries between these two lakes, but good luck getting to the ripest fruits before the local wildlife.

When I was young and invincible, I'd boulder-hop from Ringbone up the drainage to Romeo and eventually Willow Lake. These days I prefer to take the Circle Park Loop Trail (Hike 4) above Rainy Lake to reach this rock-encrusted lake.

Looking down on Long Lake

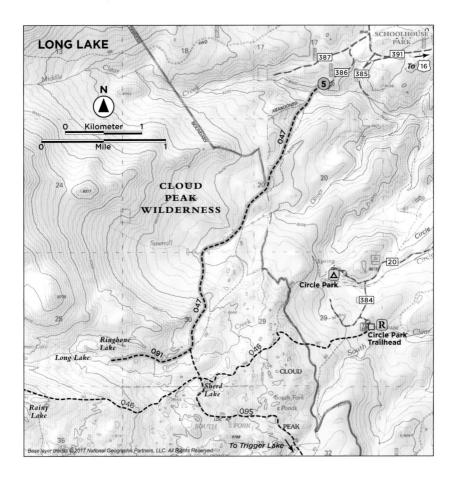

MILES AND DIRECTIONS

0.0 Trailhead. Ford Middle Clear Creek.

1.0 Trail enters Cloud Peak Wilderness.

1.6 Trail crosses Sawmill Creek.

2.5 Junction. Turn right onto Trail 091 to Long Lake. Trail 047 continues straight to Sherd Lake.

3.0 Long Lake.

6. LAKE ANGELINE, TRAIL 088

WHY GO?

This is an impressive hike to one of the larger backcountry lakes nestled over 10,500 feet high in the alpine tundra. Lake Angeline makes for a great destination if you only have a night but want to feel like you're really getting away. Spanning 2,500 feet in elevation, this hike is a lesson in habitat zones.

THE RUNDOWN

Distance: 11.6 miles out-and-back

Elevation gain: 2,503 feet

Difficulty: Strenuous due to elevation gains and distance

Hiking time: About 8 hours

Best seasons: Summer, early fall

Fees and permits: Free Cloud Peak Wilderness Use Registration

Trail contacts: Bighorn National Forest, 2013 Eastside 2nd St., Sheridan, WY 82801, (307) 674-2600, http://www.fs.usda.gov/bighorn

Maps: USDA Forest Service Bighorn National Forest, National Geographic Trails Unlimited 720 Cloud Peak Wilderness, USGS Hunter Mesa, USGS Lake Angeline

Dog-friendly: Dogs must be under control

Trail surface: Uneven terrain

Nearest town: Buffalo, Wyoming

Other trail users: ATVs until the wilderness boundary

Special considerations: There is no trail registration box at the trailhead; therefore, you'll have to obtain the free permit elsewhere, either at the Forest Service office in Buffalo or at a nearby trailhead like Hunter or Circle Park.

FINDING THE TRAILHEAD

From Buffalo, head west on US Hwy. 16. Take the exit for Schoolhouse Park/Hunter Corrals. Follow the lesser road (FR 391). Keep right as you pass intersections with FR 385 and FR 387. About 4 miles of rough and tumble roads from the highway, you'll reach FR 391/FR 398 split. The roads quickly become even nastier from here, so it is recommended to park at this junction. **Trailhead GPS:** N44 18.431' / W107 01.199'

THE HIKE

It is wise to park in the southern end of Weber Park at the intersection of FR 391 and FR 398. No need to tear up the road or your vehicle on the rocky ruts that claim to be the final stretch of FR 391. As you head west, you'll notice the theme for this hike is walking uphill through the Lost Fire Burn of 1988. Lodgepole pines now stand as healthy reminders that fire is an essential process in this landscape. Lodgepole pines have serotinous cones that are dependent on fire to release the tree seeds. The aptly named fireweed and other flowers grow readily in the years following a burn. Lodgepole saplings often grow back in thick dog-hair stands, taking decades to reach enough height to provide shade for hikers.

FR 391 is a 1.7-mile stretch that ends at the Cloud Peak Wilderness boundary. Next, you crest a ridge before dropping down into the actual wilderness area. Trail 088 continues through the heart of the Lost Fire Burn, and after another mile, the trail approaches Middle Clear Creek. You remain on the north side of the water and continue to gain elevation.

As you hike higher and higher, eventually you enter the subalpine zone. Camping is more appealing here below timberline, rather than closer to Lake Angeline. Four miles into the hike, you'll reach the now closed trail that used to connect to the Seven Brothers Lakes. Stay on the westward course. The trees become windswept and krummholz, their branches flagged by the prevailing winds which are common at these altitudes.

The final leg of this hike is above timberline. Fragile alpine cushion plants and fields of boulders define the sense of place. Snowfields linger in these parts, and the waters of Lake Angeline never get much warmer than these drifts. Cutthroat trout manage to eke out a living in these alpine waters.

Lake Angeline
CHARLES HUBBELL

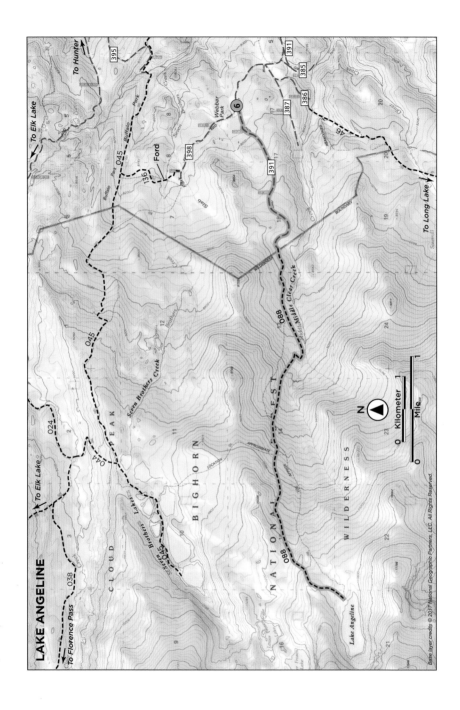

Approaching Lake Angeline
CHARLES HUBBELL

MILES AND DIRECTIONS

0.0   Park in Weber Park at FR 391/FR 398 junction.

1.7   Road ends at Cloud Peak Wildness boundary.

2.7   Trail approaches Middle Clear Creek.

4.0   Junction with abandoned trail to Seven Brothers Lakes. Stay left.

5.8   Lake Angeline.

7. SEVEN BROTHERS LAKES, TRAIL 045

WHY GO?

Don't let the heavy use discourage you. Seven Brothers is a worthy destination. With a string of seven lakes, fishing is the main draw. There is ample camping, and with so many good fishing places, you can usually find a somewhat secluded place to cast a line.

THE RUNDOWN

Distance: 5.6 miles one-way to first lake, 1.4 miles more to final lake, out-and-back or circuit

Elevation gain: 1,760 feet

Difficulty: Moderate due to distance, elevation gain, uneven footing

Hiking time: About 7 hours

Best seasons: Early summer, late fall

Fees and permits: Free Cloud Peak Wilderness Use Registration

Trail contacts: Bighorn National Forest, 2013 Eastside 2nd St., Sheridan, WY 82801, (307) 674-2600, http://www.fs.usda.gov/bighorn

Maps: USDA Forest Service Bighorn National Forest, National Geographic Trails Unlimited 720 Cloud Peak Wilderness, USGS Hunter Mesa, USGS Lake Angeline

Dog-friendly: Dogs must be under control

Trail surface: Uneven trail, primitive road

Nearest town: Buffalo, Wyoming

Other trail users: Equestrians, ATVs until wilderness boundary

FINDING THE TRAILHEAD

Take Hunter Corral/Schoolhouse Park Exit off of US Hwy. 16. Keep right onto FR 19. You'll drive past the North Fork Picnic Area as well as the Hunter Work Station. Take a left onto FR 396. You'll find ample parking at the trailhead and campground. Registration is required at the trailhead as this hike enters the Cloud Peak Wilderness.

Trailhead GPS: N44 20.300' / W106 58.587'

THE HIKE

In addition to this route to Seven Brothers Lakes via Buffalo Park and Trail 045, the destination can be reached from Soldier Park (Trail 24) and Trail 044 (for more information on this route, see Hike 8 Florence Pass). Another option for this hike is combining the routes into a loop hike traveling in from Buffalo Park and out along Soldier Park.

After registering at the trailhead, begin hiking by continuing along FR 396. Shortly, and before the road makes an impressive creek crossing, you'll turn left onto FR 394. (Note the National Geographic Cloud Peak Wilderness Map has this labeled as FR 395, but the road sign is FR 394). You'll also see the Ditch Trail (Trail 160) heading into the woods at this intersection. Hike the road for a mile to reach the fork of FR 394 and FR 395. You'll want to take the left fork for FR 395. Another mile of mostly downhill road walking brings you to the start of Trail 045. You might be able to rock-hop across the North Fork of Clear Creek, and the ford should never be more than about knee deep.

The trail continues to follow Buffalo Park, although you'll notice the elevation starts to gain following the creek crossing. The views of the peaks beckon you onward. During June, Buffalo Park is full of lupine. More common on the prairies below than in the mountains, western meadowlarks can be heard singing here in the open fields of Buffalo Park. The grasses tickle your shins as you hike for about 0.75 mile to reach the faint Buffalo Park Cutoff Trail (Trail 136). This side trail goes to Slab Park near the end of FR 398 off of Schoolhouse Park. This is a fairly miserable road, and as a result this trail sees little use.

Continuing on Trail 045 for another 0.5 mile brings you to the Cloud Peak Wilderness boundary. At the wilderness boundary, you'll begin hiking through lodgepole pine stands growing in thick following the 1988 Lost Fire. The trail gets markedly rougher here as it continues to climb. Gaps in the trees offer up impressive views of the peaks, including Ant Hill to the north, as well as sweeping looks back to the east. Pockets of timber that survived the 1988 burn offer up some welcome shade as you approach the intersection with Trail 044 and the first of the Seven Brothers Lakes.

Trail 044 hops over the ridge to the north and then drops down into the Clear Creek Drainage, connecting with Trail 024 and eventually to Soldier Park. This route makes a nice loop option from Hunter Trailhead.

Trail 045 continues up to the head of Seven Brothers Lake 6. Here a sign marks "Revegetation Project Closed to Camping and Horse Beyond this Point." Numerous paths weave in and out connecting the lakes. The scenic beauty of Seven Brothers is classic. The lakes sit on a shelf at about 9,500 feet elevation while the imposing granite domes tower some 2,000 feet higher. The best views are from a grassy knoll overlooking Lake 6. Good fishing can be had at any of the lakes. Finding a rock to perch on can help keep your backcast out of the trees if you're fly-fishing.

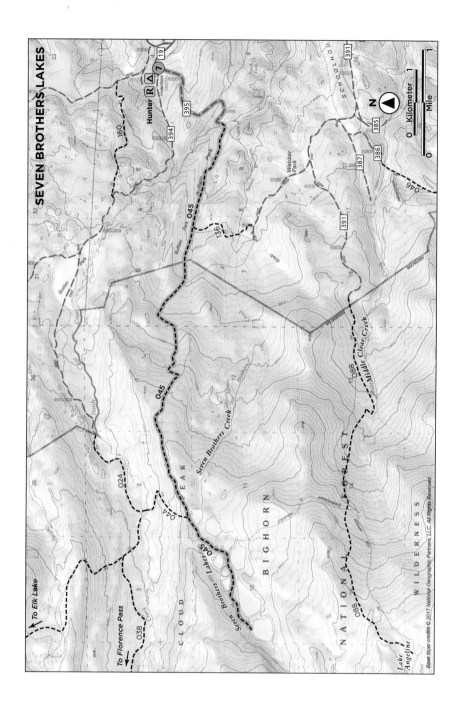

SEVEN BROTHERS LAKES

The first of the Seven Brothers Lakes

MILES AND DIRECTIONS

0.0   Hunter Trailhead.

0.1   FR 394 and Ditch Trail.

1.0   FR 394 / FR 395 split.

2.0   North Clear Creek, start of Trail 045.

3.5   Enter Cloud Peak Wilderness.

5.6   First Seven Brothers Lake and Trail 044.

7.0   Last Seven Brothers Lake.

8. FLORENCE PASS, TRAILS 024 & 038

WHY GO?

One of the most iconic hikes in the Bighorns, this pass bisects the southern end of the mountain range. The rugged canyon east of Florence Pass proper is spectacular. Most hikers use the West Tensleep Lake and Hunter Trailheads for this point-to-point thru-hike adventure.

THE RUNDOWN

Distance: 14.5 miles one-way, point-to-point, out-and-back, or circuit

Elevation gain: 3,070 feet

Difficulty: Strenuous due to elevation and distance

Hiking time: About 17 hours

Best seasons: Summer, early fall

Fees and permits: Free Cloud Peak Wilderness Use Registration

Trail contacts: Bighorn National Forest, 2013 Eastside 2nd St., Sheridan, WY 82801, (307) 674-2600, http://www.fs.usda.gov/bighorn

Maps: USDA Forest Service Bighorn National Forest, National Geographic Trails Unlimited 720 Cloud Peak Wilderness, USGS Hunter Mesa, USGS Lake Angeline, USGS Lake Helen

Dog-friendly: Dogs must be under control

Trail surface: Uneven terrain, primitive road

Nearest town: Buffalo, Wyoming

Other trail users: Equestrians, ATVs on roads until wilderness boundary

FINDING THE TRAILHEAD

Take Hunter Corral/Schoolhouse Park Exit off of US Hwy. 16. Keep right onto FR 19. You'll drive past the North Fork Picnic Area as well as the Hunter Work Station. Take a left onto FR 396. You'll find ample parking at the trailhead and campground. Registration is required at the trailhead as this hike enters the Cloud Peak Wilderness.

Trailhead GPS: N44 20.300' / W106 58.587'

THE HIKE

Florence Pass is a steady climb from Hunter in the east to Mistymoon Lake in the west. The initial elevation gain is more grueling when hiking up to Mistymoon

Fortress Lakes near Florence Pass.
TIM FEATHERS

and over the pass from the west, but beyond this, the trail continues to lose elevation at a steady pace when traveling east.

Keeping in mind that beyond the trailhead is a few miles of primitive road walking along FR 394 to the Cloud Peak Wilderness boundary, the Hunter Trailhead provides good access to the backcountry for compact cars with little clearance.

Initially this hike is the same as the beginning of the Ant Hill Hike (Hike 9). Register at the Hunter Trailhead. Start the hike by continuing along FR 396. After a quarter of a mile, hang a left. Note that some maps have this road intersection labeled as FR 395, but the road signage is FR 394. Hikers can take the 1.2-mile Ditch Trail (Trail 160). The other option is to walk the roads, which adds 0.6 mile or so to where the Ditch Trail and FR 394 meet up again. I'd suggest the trail.

A quarter of a mile west of this convergence you'll find a pair of graves. The older dates to 1877 and marks Pierre Garde, a Frenchman who was serving with a surveying party. He accidently shot himself while cleaning his gun. The second belongs to a Swedish lumberjack named Carl Johnson who passed away of natural causes in 1922. The gravesites overlook willows flanking Clear Creek in the foreground, while the towering peaks of Ant Hill, Bomber Mountain, Mather Peaks, and Darton Peak loom above Soldier Park in the distance. Florence Canyon and Pass is the notch visible in the west.

Continue hiking the road, which gets progressively rockier and worse as it pushes westward. You'll enter the trees again for the final stretch of road, reaching the Cloud Peak Wilderness boundary and Trail 024.

Beyond the wilderness boundary, the meadows of Trail Park eventually open up. About 1.1 miles from the end of the road, Trail 44 heads south and crosses the North Fork of Clear Creek before climbing up and over the ridge and dropping down to Seven Brothers Lakes (Hike 7).

Meanwhile, Trail 024 continues charting westward through Trail Park. Half a mile later, Trail 024 dead ends at Trail 038, the Solitude Loop Trail. The Florence Pass segment lies ahead to the west. The Ant Hill segment is to the north (Hike 9).

The trail stays mostly in the trees for a bit. One and three quarter miles beyond the Ant Hill Trail intersection, Trail 038 crosses over to the south side of Clear Creek. Before the crossing, you could follow the open meadow to the north/northeast for a glimpse at Deer Lake. This would also make a solid campsite, slightly removed from the trail.

As the elevation gains, the forest makes the transition from lodgepole pine to the subalpine timbers of Engelmann spruce, limber pine, and subalpine fir. The mountain cliffs start to close in around you as you push onward. Avalanche chutes

Florence Pass from Trail Park

and melting trickles of snow serve as a reminder that spring comes late at these elevations.

The trail returns to the north banks of North Clear Creek after about a mile, eventually reaching Powell Creek, a small tributary stream coming in from the north. From here, the incline increases through Medicine Park and the narrow gorge of Florence Canyon. Look for waterfalls cascading off the mountain faces.

Rocks dominate the landscape as the path weaves through the alpine tundra. The coolness in the air is felt year-round. Scamper over three easy rock-hops back and forth across North Clear Creek as it empties from Florence Lake.

The flanks of Bomber Mountain loom over Florence Lake. Look for the memorial commemorating the tragic 1943 plane crash of a World War II B-17 Bomber

Mistymoon Lake from Florence Pass Trail

that was flying from Oregon to Nebraska. Parts of the wreckage can still be seen reflecting in the sun directly north of the lake. While there is no official trail up Bomber Mountain, many people venture north of Florence Lake to visit the site of the wreckage and to pay respect to the ten men who lost their lives in the crash.

Next, the trail reaches the highest point along the entire Solitude Loop Trail, Florence Pass, just shy of 11,000 feet in elevation. The descent of the west side of the pass is steep and rocky. The trail runs north of Gunboat Lake and splits between the Fortress Lakes. The final pitch downward leads to Mistymoon Lake. From here, Trail 063 heads south for the West Tensleep Lake Trailhead (Hike 15). The Solitude Trail wraps around the western end of Mistymoon where it intersects Trail 066, which follows Middle Paint Rock Creek (Hike 16). The Solitude Loop Trail continues onward to Lake Solitude (Hike 17).

MILES AND DIRECTIONS

0.0 Hunter Trailhead.

0.1 FR 394 and Ditch Trail.

1.0 FR 394/FR 395 split.

1.8 Bridge over Clear Creek.

2.4 Graves.

4.6 Cloud Peak Wilderness. Start of Trail 024.

5.7 Junction with Trail 044 cutoff to Seven Brothers Lakes.

6.2 Intersection with Solitude Loop (Trail 038). Bear left. Hike 9 to Elk Lake is to the right.

7.9 Cross to south bank of North Clear Creek.

9.0 Ford North Clear Creek.

9.9 Trail crosses Powell Creek.

10.5 Medicine Park.

12.0 First of three fords of North Clear Creek.

12.7 Florence Pass.

13.4 Trail crosses Gunboat Lake outlet.

13.7 Fortress Lakes.

14.5 Mistymoon Lake.

14.7 Junction with Mistymoon (Hike 15) and Lake Solitude (Hike 17) Trails.

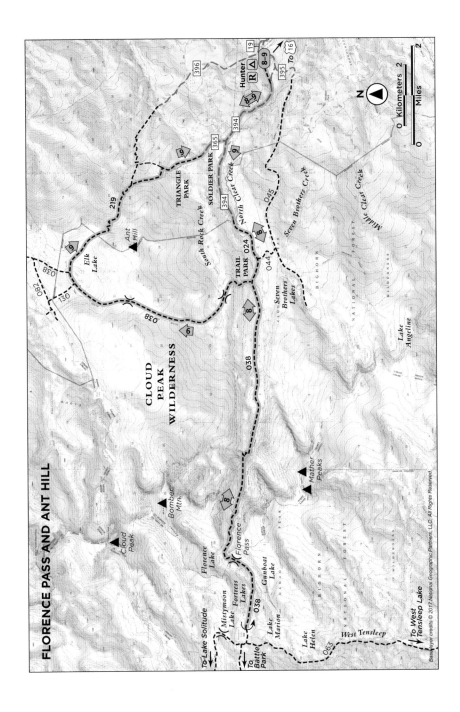

FLORENCE PASS AND ANT HILL

CLOUD PEAK WILDERNESS

BIGHORN NATIONAL FOREST

WILDERNESS

9. ANT HILL, TRAILS 024 & 038

WHY GO?

This trail travels through some of the prettiest terrain in the Bighorn Mountains. It can be the first leg of a Solitude Loop adventure. It can also make for a nice overnight backpack loop from the Hunter Trailhead when coupled with the Elk Lake Trail (Trail 219).

THE RUNDOWN See map on page 55.

Distance: 5.3 miles circuit from Florence Pass Trail to Reservoirs Trail, 11.5 miles one-way out-and-back from Hunter Trailhead

Elevation gain: 2,600 feet

Difficulty: Strenuous due to elevation gains, distance, and uneven terrain

Hiking time: About 3.5 hours

Best seasons: Summer, fall

Fees and permits: Free Cloud Peak Wilderness Use Registration

Trail contacts: Bighorn National Forest, 2013 Eastside 2nd St.,Sheridan, WY 82801, (307)

674-2600, http://www.fs.usda .gov/bighorn

Maps: USDA Forest Service Bighorn National Forest, National Geographic Trails Unlimited 720 Cloud Peak Wilderness, USGS Hunter Mesa, USGS Lake Angeline, USGS Willow Park Reservoir

Dog-friendly: Dogs must be under control

Trail surface: Uneven terrain

Nearest town: Buffalo, Wyoming

Other trail users: Equestrians, ATVs on roads until wilderness boundary

---

FINDING THE TRAILHEAD

Take Hunter Corral/Schoolhouse Park Exit off of US Hwy. 16. Keep right onto FR 19. You'll drive past the North Fork Picnic Area as well as the Hunter Work Station. Take a left onto FR 396. You'll find ample parking at the trailhead and campground. Registration is required at the trailhead as this hike enters the Cloud Peak Wilderness.

Trailhead GPS: N44 19.920' / W106 59.363' at Florence Pass Trail
N44 20.300' / W106 58.587' at Hunter Trailhead

THE HIKE

Along the Solitude Loop (Trail 038), this segment is the linkage between Florence Pass Trail (see Hike 8) and the Reservoirs (Hike 24).

Soldier Park Graves

Keeping in mind that the trailhead is a couple of miles of primitive road walking from the Cloud Peak Wilderness boundary, the Hunter Trailhead provides good access to the backcountry for compact cars with little clearance.

Initially, this hike is the same as the lower stretches of Florence Pass (Hike 8). Register at the Hunter Trailhead. Start the hike by continuing along FR 396. After a quarter of a mile, hang a left. Note, the National Geographic map has this road intersection labeled as FR 395, but the road signage is FR 394. Hikers can take the 1.2-mile Ditch Trail (Trail 160). The other option is to walk the roads, which adds 0.6 mile or so to where the Ditch Trail and FR 394 meet up again. I'd suggest the trail. A quarter of a mile west of this convergence, you'll find a pair of graves. (See Hike 8 Florence Pass for more information on the graves.)

The meadow of Soldier Park proper opens up beyond the graves, revealing views of Florence Canyon cutting between Mather Peaks and Bomber Mountain roughly 10 miles in the distance. Ant Hill is a noticeable presence as well.

Continue hiking the road, which gets progressively rockier and worse as it pushes westward. You'll enter the trees again for the final stretch of road, reaching the Cloud Peak Wilderness boundary and Trail 024. The meadows of Trail Park eventually open up. Beyond the wilderness boundary, about 1.1 miles from the end of the road, Trail 44 heads south and crosses the North Fork of Clear Creek before climbing up and over the ridge and dropping down to Seven Brothers Lakes (Hike 7). Meanwhile, Trail 024 continues charting westward through Trail Park. In season, prairie smoke (aka old man's whiskers), asters, and pussytoes line the trail. Half a mile later, Trail 024 dead ends at Trail 038, the Solitude Loop Trail. The Florence Pass segment lies ahead to the west, while the Ant Hill segment heads north (to the right).

The Ant Hill trail segment climbs up and over a lateral moraine, piles of rock rubble that accumulated to the sides as glaciers carved out the valley. Then it works west along the southern banks of South Rock Creek for about three quarters of a mile, before fording the creek and climbing north up the western slopes of Ant Hill. The trail eventually crests the saddle before dropping to Elk Lake. Near the divide, alpine tundra and rock outcroppings replace the timbers found at lower elevations. Look for marmots sunning themselves on large boulders, or listen for their pure whistling chirps.

Nestled in a shallow depression, Elk Lake makes for a stunning panorama as the granite peaks rise above, none standing taller than Cloud Peak.

Trail 130 offers an option to cut over to Flatiron Lake and Cloud Peak Reservoir (along Trail 082). The Solitude Trail continues to the eastern outlet of Elk Lake before turning north to The Reservoirs (Hike 24) including Willow Park and Kearny Lake Reservoirs, and eventually to Lake Winnie (Hike 23).

Hikers looking to return to Hunter Trailhead can retrace their steps along the western side of Ant Hill, or they can opt to head southeast from Elk Lake along Trail 219, eventually coming to FR 365, and then back to Soldier Park.

MILES AND DIRECTIONS

0.0   Trail departs from Florence Pass Trail.

0.5   Top of initial grade.

1.3   Trail fords South Rock Creek.

2.9   Pass below Ant Hill.

4.4   Trail reaches head of Elk Lake.

4.7   Trail departs for Cloud Peak Reservoir. Bear right.

5.3   Foot of Elk Lake. Junction with Elk Lake and Reservoirs (Hike 24) Trails.

BUFFALO AND SOUTHEAST WILDERNESS ACCESS ADDITIONAL HIKES

Elk Lake Trail (Trail 219) connects Soldier Park with Elk Lake. When coupled with Ant Hill (Trail 038, Hike 9), it can make a nice loop from Hunter Trailhead. The South Rock Creek Trail (Trail 041, Hike 26) also connects with the Elk Lake Trail.

Pole Creek Nordic Ski Trail (Trail 557) begins and ends at a parking lot off of FR 457. It offers nearly 11 miles of groomed trails in the winter; however, these routes can also be hiked during the summer months.

Tie Hack Trail (Trail 107) connects Tie Hack Reservoir with the Middle Fork of Clear Creek at the YMCA Camp of the Rockies.

Tie Hack Reservoir

POWDER RIVER PASS AND WESTERN WILDERNESS ACCESS

Powder River Pass drops down to Ten Sleep, Wyoming, along the way passing high-elevation gems like Meadowlark Lake, as well as the impressive chasm of Tensleep Canyon.

The James T. Saban Lookout Tower, just west of Powder River Pass, provides a stunning overview of the western slopes of Cloud Peak and the surrounding high country.

The West Tensleep Lake region is a high use area in the Bighorns and is subject to special regulations affecting camping and waste disposal. Day trips in the area include the scenic Tensleep Falls as well as the Tensleep Trail, blazed in 2016, and providing a linkage between Island Park and Deer Park Campgrounds.

Mistymoon Lake, reached from multiple trailheads, is a crowded destination. Hikers might be wise to opt for one of the other equally as stunning lakes to establish a basecamp when exploring the high country. Many of these trails flirt with timberline, some reaching the highest talus slopes of the Bighorns. The Solitude Loop Trail travels by its namesake lake here, connecting with Coffeen Park to the north and Florence Pass to the east.

Lower Paint Rock Lake Trailhead is an out-of-the-way trailhead at the end of a long stretch of forest roads. From here, you can traverse some spectacular territory on spoke trails that connect into the Cloud Peak Wilderness via Edelman Pass or Geneva Pass.

Paint Rock Falls near
the base of Cloud Peak

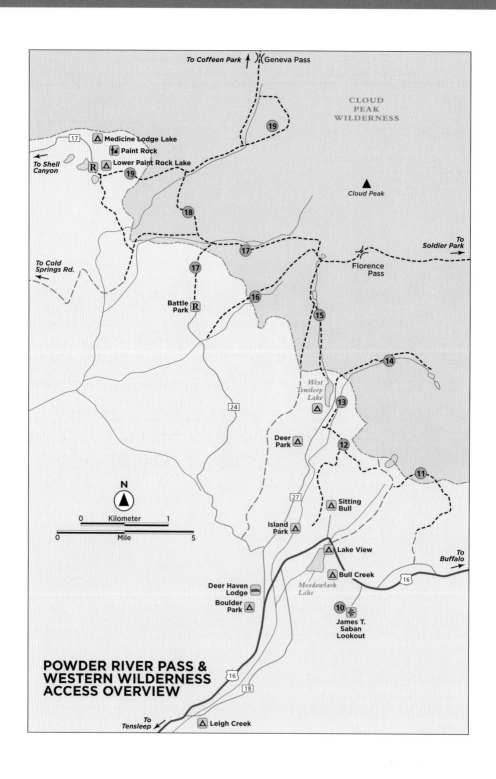

To Coffeen Park ↑)(Geneva Pass

CLOUD PEAK WILDERNESS

19

17 △ Medicine Lodge Lake
🏠 Paint Rock
To Shell Canyon
R △ Lower Paint Rock Lake
19

▲ Cloud Peak

18

17

To Cold Springs Rd.

16

To Soldier Park

Florence Pass

15

Battle Park R

14

West Tensleep Lake

13 △

24

Deer Park △

12

11

N

0   Kilometer   1
0   Mile   5

27

Sitting Bull △

Island Park △

Lake View △

To Buffalo

16

Deer Haven Lodge

Meadowlark Lake

Bull Creek △

10

Boulder Park △

James T. Saban Lookout

POWDER RIVER PASS &
WESTERN WILDERNESS
ACCESS OVERVIEW

16

18

To Tensleep

△ Leigh Creek

10. JAMES T. SABAN LOOKOUT, TRAIL 070

WHY GO?

This is a short hike to a former fire lookout tower built in 1942. The views make this a perfect trip for those crystal clear mountain bluebird sky days so common in the Bighorn Mountains.

THE RUNDOWN

Distance: 0.6 mile out-and-back

Elevation gain: 272 feet

Difficulty: Moderate due to steep grades, uneven trail including stairs

Hiking time: About 1 hour

Best seasons: Summer, fall

Fees and permits: No fees or permits required

Trail contacts: Bighorn National Forest, 2013 Eastside 2nd St., Sheridan, WY 82801, (307)

674-2600, http://www.fs.usda.gov/bighorn

Maps: USDA Forest Service Bighorn National Forest, USGS Meadowlark Lake, USGS Onion Gulch

Dog-friendly: Dogs must be under control

Trail surface: Uneven terrain, stairs

Nearest town: Ten Sleep, Wyoming

Other trail users: None

FINDING THE TRAILHEAD

Take US Hwy. 16 to between Meadowlark Lake and Powder River Pass. Look for the signs for the "St. Christopher's in the Bighorns chapel for travelers." From this point, drive south on FR 429. Drive past FR 433 to the right and FR 434 to the left. Just beyond this, about a mile from the highway, take the big bend in the road to the right and continue up the hill. You'll find parking at the edge of the trees.

Trailhead GPS: N44 09.068' / W107 12.086'

THE HIKE

You'll see the former lookout tower perched among the rocky jumble at the top of the ridge as you drive in. It doesn't seem like much of a lofty perch, until you remember you'll have to climb this hill. It's a short but steep walk. At the top, enjoy vast views stretching from the prairies to the high peaks. Meadowlark Lake looks like a painting from this vantage point, and wildlife can often be spotted grazing in distant meadows.

Formerly known as the High Park Lookout, the James T. Saban Lookout was rededicated on June 20, 2015. Mr. Saban was a Forest Service ranger from nearby Hyattville, Wyoming. He served as Civilian Conservation Corps foreman at Tensleep Camp F-35. In August 1937, James T. Saban, along with fourteen other men, died while fighting the Blackwater Fire in the Shoshone National Forest.

The hike starts at the parking lot in the edge of the trees. The trailhead is marked with a sign reading "Visitors Welcomed 15 Minute Walk," although don't expect anyone to welcome you. This lookout tower is rarely in service these days.

The trail (Trail 070) leads through the forest over rocky and uneven terrain. Part of the elevation gained on this hike is courtesy of nearly one hundred stairs. There is a log bench about half way up, and there is no shame in stopping for a water break. Chipmunks run about, and piles of pinecone scales accumulate in red squirrel middens. Elk sign is common here as well.

Looking below you'll see the "High Park Range Study Plot Established 1953" that you past on the drive in. From the top, try and pick out mule deer in High Park below. They are sure to be hiding in the sagebrush, which is just tall enough to obscure a bedded down deer. The only thing obstructing your views of Bighorn Peak is a violet-green swallow darting by with regularity.

Looking southeast, you see the Leigh Creek drainage and Pasture Park beyond. Pasture Park makes a lovely stroll (Trails 410, 412, and 413) when the wildflowers are in peak bloom. Leigh Creek is a lasting tribute to Englishman Gilbert Leigh who met an untimely death in nearby Tensleep Canyon in 1884. Leigh stepped away from his hunting camp one night, and unfortunately tumbled over the edge of the cliff.

Originally known as High Point Lookout, the tower was built in 1942 and is an L4 design structure. It is 14 square feet and is surrounded by a catwalk. There are large windows on all four sides. Shutters act as awnings when raised and protect the windows when lowered. Fire spotters lived in the tower during fire season. Bunks, cabinets, tables, shelves, and wood stoves were all constructed low as to not block the view from the Osborne Fire Finder that occupied the middle of the room.

While it is worth the hike, this is the last place I'd want to be during a lightning storm. It's a great summer or fall hike for families.

This is one of three lookout towers that remain in the Bighorns. Sheep Mountain Lookout Tower east of Powder River Pass is available for overnight rentals through the Forest Service. Black Mountain Lookout (Hike 38) is in the northern end of the Bighorns.

James T. Saban Lookout Tower
MOLLY McKAY

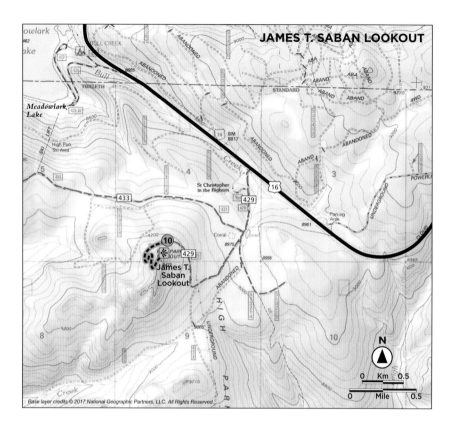

MILES AND DIRECTIONS

0.0   Trailhead.

0.3   James T. Saban Lookout Tower.

11. **LAKE MCLAIN, TRAIL 079**

WHY GO?

This hike is just 1.6 miles from the end of the road, although it might be advisable to ditch the vehicle well before the road ends. Staying on the trail can be a bit of a challenge, but Bighorn Peak towering over Lake McLain makes this a scenic adventure.

THE RUNDOWN

Distance: 3.2 miles out-and-back

Elevation gain: 420 feet

Difficulty: Moderate due to inclines and uneven trail surface

Hiking time: About 2 hours

Best seasons: Summer

Fees and permits: Free Cloud Peak Wilderness Use Registration

Trail contacts: Bighorn National Forest, 2013 Eastside 2nd St., Sheridan, WY 82801, (307) 674-2600, http://www.fs.usda.gov/bighorn

Maps: USDA Forest Service Bighorn National Forest, National Geographic Trails Unlimited 720 Cloud Peak Wilderness, and USGS Meadowlark Lake

Dog-friendly: Dogs must be under control

Trail surface: Uneven terrain, boulders

Nearest town: Ten Sleep, Wyoming

Other trail users: None

Special considerations: Maps have been switching Maybelle Lake and Lake McLain for years. Current information indicates that McLain is the larger one to the west, with Maybelle to the east. Maps have also mislabeled this as Trail 078 in the past.

FINDING THE TRAILHEAD

Take US Hwy. 16 to Meadowlark Lake. Between the Sitting Bull and Lakeview turns (about 0.2 mile west of Meadowlark Lodge), FR 430 heads northeast. This rough and rutted road isn't suitable for low clearance vehicles, and it turns into a mud bog at the thought of rain. There are adequate pullouts right off the highway. The road runs along East Tensleep Creek for 3 miles to the trailhead. Park here at the base of a rocky grade and the signpost marked "McLain Trail." Note the "road" turns north and continues on, eventually ending up near East Tensleep Lake.

Trailhead GPS: N44 12.459' / W107 09.773'

THE HIKE

This trail enters the Cloud Peak Wilderness, but there isn't a registration box at the trailhead. Before setting off for this hike, you should register at a ranger station, Forest Service office, or one of the other trailheads.

This hike is 1.6 miles from FR 430. The road is pretty sketchy right off the highway, but beyond that, slow and careful driving should get you to the start of the trail. This is a road I wouldn't drive a rental car on, and I'd prefer not to drive my own car on it. But I'd be pretty comfortable driving a buddy's vehicle over it.

This footpath ascends in short burst to reach a picturesque lake at the foot of Bighorn Peak. The trail can be faint in a few spots. Look for cairn and blazes as you travel along. Maps have been switching Lake McLain with Maybelle Lake for years. Current information suggests that McLain is the larger one to the west, with Maybelle to the east.

From the sign marked "McLain Trail," follow the trail marker posts eastward along the edge of a grassy meadow. The trail (Trail 079, although some maps have it labeled at Trail 078) becomes more obvious as it moves inside the trees. As the path climbs steadily, willows replace grasses in the clearings. Look for moose in the willow, as this is one of their favorite snacks. Bighorn Peak rises ahead.

The path soon rock-hops across a small stream. Here you'll enter the Cloud Peak Wilderness. The trail then crosses rocky glades among the spruce trees and continues following the stream to a boggy crossing. A level trek then leads to a round, lush sedge meadow. After skirting it, the path climbs the final pitch through a wooded draw to reach Lake McLain. This deep-water gem is surrounded by subalpine forest.

There is an option to continue over the ridge and down into marshy ringed Maybelle Lake. Maps also show the trail leading onward to Baby Wagon Creek. These trails are faint at best in many sections and a proliferation of cairns also leads to confusion.

Lake McLain
CHARLES HUBBELL

Lake McLain Trailhead
CHARLES HUBBELL

Lake McLain
CHARLES HUBBELL

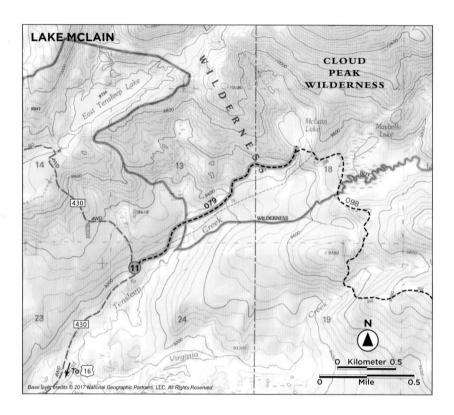

MILES AND DIRECTIONS

0.0 McLain Trail trailhead.

0.6 Trail crosses substantial stream.

1.0 Second stream crossing.

1.6 Lake McLain.

12. TENSLEEP TRAIL, TRAIL 156

WHY GO?

Folks often associate the West Tensleep Lake as the trailhead to Mistymoon Lake, but there are plenty of other hiking options in the area as well. The Tensleep Trail was constructed in the summer of 2016. It connects Island Park Campground to the High Line Trail near Deer Park Campground. You can make a short day trip out of the trails, or you can extend the trip along the High Line all the way to East Tensleep Lake for a loop trip or an overnight stay.

THE RUNDOWN

Distance: 2.8 miles one-way, point-to-point, out-and-back, or circuit

Elevation gain: Minimal

Difficulty: Moderate due to uneven footing

Hiking time: About 1 hour

Best seasons: Spring, summer, fall

Fees and permits: No fees or permits are required

Trail contacts: Bighorn National Forest, 2013 Eastside 2nd St., Sheridan, WY 82801, (307) 674-2600, http://www.fs.usda.gov/bighorn

Maps: USDA Forest Service Bighorn National Forest, National Geographic Trails Unlimited

720 Cloud Peak Wilderness, USGS Lake Helen, USGS Meadowlark Lake

Dog-friendly: Dogs must be under control

Trail surface: Uneven terrain

Nearest town: Ten Sleep, Wyoming

Other trail users: Mountain bikers

Special considerations: The West Tensleep area is subject to restrictions on dispersed camping and regulations that all human waste must be packed out. This is essential to provide positive recreation experiences and protect the natural resources in areas of high use such as this.

FINDING THE TRAILHEAD

US Hwy. 16 goes by Deer Haven Lodge to the west of Meadowlark Lake. Take FR 27 north to go past Deer Haven. While this road has heavy washboarding, it remains a very passable road. Stay on FR 27 to reach the Deer Park Campground. Continue on FR 27 to cross the bridge. Parking is available for a couple of vehicles at the wide pullout on the east side of the road. Parking at Deer Park is another option. The trail takes off from here at the High Line Trailhead.

Trailhead GPS: N44 14.682' / W107 13.231'

Middle Tensleep Creek

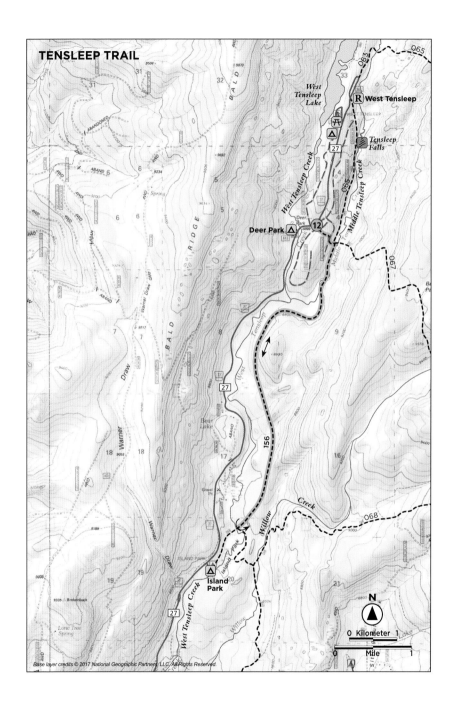

THE HIKE

The Tensleep Trail was constructed during the summer of 2016. It makes a nice addition to the network of trails in the West Tensleep Lake corridor. The trail can be hiked as a daytrip from Island Park or Deer Park Campgrounds.

There are a couple of parking spots in a wide spot off the road to West Tensleep Lake. Parking is on the east side of the road right after crossing the bridge to the north of Deer Park Campground. Parking near the campground is another option. The Tensleep Trail (Trail 156) shares the trailhead with the High Line Trail (Trail 067) here. Head east into the woods for about a half a mile to reach a sturdy bridge crossing over Middle Tensleep Creek. The Tensleep Falls Trail (Hike 13) heads north from the west side of the bridge. Shortly after the bridge, the Tensleep Trail splits off to the right (south) from the High Line Trail.

The Tensleep Trail sticks to the eastern side of Middle Tensleep Creek for much of the hike. Elk sign is abundant in the area, although these large critters are more elusive than you might think. Consider yourself lucky if you spot a bull with summer antlers still fuzzy with velvet or a small herd of cows and spotted calves grazing in a meadow clearing. Nearly black in color, moose are also common in the drainage. Moose can be seen anywhere from here all the way up to Mistymoon Lake.

The southern end of the Tensleep Trail connects with Trail 068 close to Island Park Campground. Trail 068 runs from near the Tyrrell Workstation northeast to East Tensleep Lake. There are multiple unauthorized trails that make sticking to the main trail a bit tricky in a few sections of Trail 068, but better signage and recent trail maintenance are helping to improve this.

The Tensleep Trail can be approached as an out-and-back day hike from Island Park or Deer Park Campgrounds. It makes a nice extension when added to the Tensleep Falls Hike (Trail 065, Hike 13). It can also be treated as a loop hike when coupled with Trails 067 and 068. Overall, it is an outstanding addition to the area—sure to become a favorite with hikers of all abilities.

MILES AND DIRECTIONS

0.0 High Line Trailhead off of FR 27 near Deer Park Campground.

0.5 Bridge over Middle Tensleep Creek. Hike 13 heads north to Tensleep Falls on the west side of the creek. Beyond the bridge, the Tensleep Trail (Trail 156) heads south from High Line Trail.

2.8 Tensleep Trail intersects with Trail 068 near Island Park Campground.

13. TENSLEEP FALLS, TRAIL 065

WHY GO?
Waterfalls are not an abundant resource in the Bighorn Mountains; however, Tensleep Falls is one notable feature. The 20-foot falls are an easy stroll from West Tensleep Lake, so next time the fish aren't biting you can check them out. The falls are also a short walk from Deer Park Campground.

THE RUNDOWN

Distance: 0.7 mile one-way to falls out-and-back

Elevation gain: 265 feet

Difficulty: Easy due to short distance

Hiking time: About 1 hour

Best seasons: Late spring, summer, fall

Fees and permits: No fees or permits required

Trail contacts: Bighorn National Forest, 2013 Eastside 2nd St., Sheridan, WY 82801, (307) 674-2600, http://www.fs.usda.gov/bighorn

Maps: USDA Forest Service Bighorn National Forest, National Geographic Trails Unlimited 720

Cloud Peak Wilderness, USGS Lake Helen, USGS Meadowlark Lake

Dog-friendly: Dogs must be under control

Trail surface: Uneven terrain

Nearest town: Ten Sleep, Wyoming

Other trail users: None

Special considerations: The West Tensleep area is subject to restrictions on dispersed camping and regulations that all human waste must be packed out. This is essential to provide positive recreation experiences and protect the natural resources in areas of high use such as this.

FINDING THE TRAILHEAD
US Hwy. 16 travels by Deer Haven Lodge to the west of Meadowlark Lake. Take FR 27 to the north to go past Deer Haven. While this road has heavy washboarding, it remains a very passable road. Stay on FR 27 for 8 miles as you pass Tyrell Work Station and Island Park, Deer Park, and West Tensleep Campgrounds, as well as numerous private cabins. The West Tensleep Trailhead is at the end of the road.
Trailhead GPS: N44 15.679' / W107 12.765'

THE HIKE

Tensleep Falls are about equidistant from West Tensleep Lake and Deer Park Campground. Most folks hike this as an out-and-back, although you could run a shuttle vehicle easy enough. From the West Tensleep Lake area, the trail takes off near the southeast corner of the long-term parking lot.

Tensleep Falls

From the parking lot, the trail (Trail 065) parallels the western bank of Middle Tensleep Creek along a pine ridge. You're hiking upstream of the falls initially. After about three quarters of a mile, a spur trail drops down to the water's edge. This puts you below the falls. Looking back upstream, you see the stream plunging over a sheer drop of 20+ feet. While far from the largest falls out there, Tensleep Falls is a pretty destination. The easy hike makes it great for families, and it is a hike that can be repeated throughout the seasons and over the years.

Tensleep Falls from above

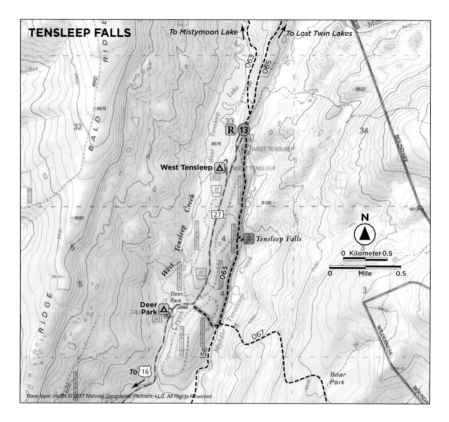

The falls make for a nice water break if you plan to continue south down the well-worn trail. About three quarters of a mile south of the falls, the trail connects to the High Line Trail (Trail 067). The Deer Park Trailhead lies 0.5 mile to the west (right). The trail comes out on FR 27 a tenth of a mile north of Deer Park Campground. If you take a left to head east at the intersection of the Tensleep Falls and High Line Trails, you can cross a sturdy bridge. From here, you can hike all of the way to East Tensleep Lake, or you can make a quick right after the bridge to head south along the newly constructed Tensleep Trail (Hike 12).

MILES AND DIRECTIONS

0.0 West Tensleep Trailhead.

0.7 Spur trail to base of falls (0.1 mile, moderate).

0.8 Junction with trail from West Tensleep Campground. Continue straight ahead.

1.5 Junction with High Line Trail. Turn right.

2.0 High Line Trailhead near Deer Park Campground.

14. LOST TWIN LAKES, TRAIL 065

WHY GO?

Lost Twin Lakes are a pair of gorgeous lakes tucked in at the base of towering summits. This trip can be done in a single day, but it is a far more enjoyable experience if you stretch it out for 2 or 3 days.

THE RUNDOWN

Distance: 12.2 out-and-back

Elevation gain: 1,490 feet

Difficulty: Strenuous due to distance and elevation gains

Hiking time: About 8 hours

Best seasons: Summer, early fall

Fees and permits: Free Cloud Peak Wilderness Use Registration

Trail contacts: Bighorn National Forest, 2013 Eastside 2nd St., Sheridan, WY 82801, (307) 674-2600, http://www.fs.usda.gov/bighorn

Maps: USDA Forest Service Bighorn National Forest, National Geographic Trails Unlimited 720 Cloud Peak Wilderness, USGS Lake Helen

Dog-friendly: Dogs must be under control

Trail surface: Uneven terrain

Nearest town: Ten Sleep, Wyoming

Other trail users: Equestrians to Mirror Lake

Special considerations: The West Tensleep area is subject to restrictions on dispersed camping and regulations that all human waste must be packed out. This is essential to provide positive recreation experiences and protect the natural resources in areas of high use such as this.

FINDING THE TRAILHEAD

US Hwy. 16 travels by Deer Haven Lodge to the west of Meadowlark Lake. Take FR 27 to the north to go past Deer Haven. While this road has heavy washboarding, it remains a very passable road. Stay on FR 27 for 8 miles as you pass Tyrell Work Station and Island Park, Deer Park, and West Tensleep Campgrounds, as well as numerous private cabins. The West Tensleep Trailhead is at the end of the road.

Trailhead GPS: N44 15.742' / W107 12.767'

THE HIKE

Since this hike enters the Cloud Peak Wilderness, you'll have to self-register. The registration box is near the parking lot.

Head north out of the West Tensleep Lake Trailhead. After just 0.1 mile, you'll reach a splitting of the trails. Bear right onto Trail 065 for Mirror and Lost Twin Lakes. (Trail 063 to the left leads to Mistymoon Lake Hike 12.) The Lost Lakes Trail gains elevation as it continues north for about a mile.

The trail heads more easterly from here. The overall elevation gain is broken up by three downhill stretches. The first drops you off a lodgepole covered medial moraine and down to Middle Tensleep Creek, which flows through a broad meadow clearing. Just before entering the Cloud Peak Wilderness, the trail passes a double waterfall above the head of the clearing.

About the time your legs feel rested from the initial climb, you'll head up again. This time you're headed up a granite knoll. From this mini-peak, take in views from the Mather Peaks in the north to Bighorn Peak in the south.

The trail dips here, crossing another meadow before taking on another steep climb up along an outlet stream. This time Mirror Lake is waiting for you as you crest the top. The trail passes along the southern shore of Mirror Lake and then again traveling along the northern side of Middle Tensleep Creek. Horses are not recommended beyond Mirror Lake.

The stretch of trail between Mirror Lake and the Lost Twin Lakes offers up suitable camping. Look for established sites well off the creek. Staying in the meadows leading up to the Lost Twin Lakes helps maintain the fragile and pristine nature of the location.

Upper Lost Twin Lake
CHARLES HUBBELL

Lower Lost Twin Lake
CHARLES HUBBELL

Lost Twin Lakes Trail near Mirror Lake
CHARLES HUBBELL

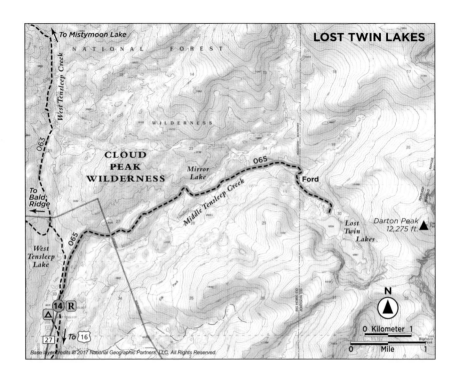

MILES AND DIRECTIONS

0.0   West Tensleep Trailhead.

0.1   Junction with Mistymoon Trail (Hike 15). Bear right.

1.5   Falls on Middle Tensleep Creek.

1.6   Trail enters Cloud Peak Wilderness.

2.9   Trail crosses the outlet of Mirror Lake.

3.3   Trail passes south shore of Mirror Lake.

5.0   Trail fords Middle Tensleep Creek.

6.1   Lost Twin Lakes.

15. MISTYMOON LAKE, TRAIL 063

WHY GO?

This is a heavily used trail and is subject to special use regulations including packing out human waste laws. Mistymoon Lake is often used as basecamp for hikers attempting to bag Cloud Peak. The location is at a crossroads of the Solitude Loop Trail. Hikers can head west to Lake Solitude and beyond or access Florence Pass to the east.

THE RUNDOWN

Distance: 7.2 miles one-way, out-and-back or circuit

Elevation gain: 970 feet

Difficulty: Strenuous due to distance, elevation gains, and uneven terrain

Hiking time: About 10 hours

Best seasons: Late spring, summer, early fall

Fees and permits: Free Cloud Peak Wilderness Use Registration

Trail contacts: Bighorn National Forest, 2013 Eastside 2nd St., Sheridan, WY 82801, (307) 674-2600, http://www.fs.usda.gov/bighorn

Maps: USDA Forest Service Bighorn National Forest, National Geographic Trails Unlimited 720 Cloud Peak Wilderness, USGS Lake Helen

Dog-friendly: Dogs must be under control

Trail surface: Uneven terrain

Nearest town: Ten Sleep, Wyoming

Other trail users: Equestrians

Special considerations: The West Tensleep area (including Mistymoon Lake) is subject to restrictions on dispersed camping and regulations that all human waste must be packed out. This is essential to provide positive recreation experiences and protect the natural resources in areas of high use such as this.

FINDING THE TRAILHEAD

US Hwy. 16 travels by Deer Haven Lodge to the west of Meadowlark Lake. Take FR 27 to the north to go past Deer Haven. While this road has heavy washboarding, it remains a very passable road. Stay on FR 27 for 8 miles as you pass Tyrell Work Station and Island Park, Deer Park, and West Tensleep Campgrounds, as well as numerous private cabins. The West Tensleep Trailhead is at the end of the road.
Trailhead GPS: N44 15.742' / W107 12.767'

THE HIKE

Expect to cross paths with a few other hiking parties on this trail, but keep in mind that even the most crowded trails in the Bighorns are hardly crowded. Make sure to register at the trailhead, even if you are only entering the wilderness for the day. The trail heads north from the West Tensleep Lake long-term parking lot.

Also note that the West Tensleep and Middle Tensleep drainages are subject to high-use restrictions, including regulations that solid human waste and used toilet paper are to be contained in leak-proof portable toilet or other self-contained receptacle and packed out of the area. This is essential for maintaining high-quality recreational experiences, while minimizing impacts including degraded water quality and other unacceptable risks to natural resources as well as for human health and safety. These regulations apply to users both within and out of the Cloud Peak Wilderness and are effective north of the Tyrell Work Station.

From the trailhead, stay on Trail 063 by keeping left 0.1 mile out of the parking lot. The right fork leads to Lost Twin Lakes (Trail 065, Hike 14). The trail remains fairly level for the first mile as you hike along the northeast side of West Tensleep Lake. Just north of the lake, at mile 1.3, the trail crosses West Tensleep Creek, and 0.1 mile later the Bald Ridge cutoff trail (Trail 064) heads west (left). Keep right to maintain Trail 063.

Over the course of the next 6 miles, the trail steadily gains nearly 1,000 feet in elevation. The trail is a mix of forested cover with the occasional mountain meadow offering up an inspiring view that keeps you motivated to continue onward and upward.

After 4.5 miles, the Bald Ridge Trail (097) joins Trail 063. Bald Ridge is a great alternative option to Lake Helen (see below). This trail parallels the main trail from atop the lateral moraine that the West Tensleep Glacier left behind.

Continue north along Trail 063 for 0.3 mile to reach the lower end of scenic Lake Helen. Lake Helen and Lake Marion get overshadowed by Mistymoon Lake, but both are impressive bodies of water. Of the three lakes, the fishing tends to be best in Lake Helen. The trail stays on the western banks of Lake Helen for nearly half a mile.

Lake Marion is less than a mile farther. Cloud Peak looms ahead up the valley. As the trail climbs, the subalpine forests start to thin out, and the rocky talus becomes more prevalent. Look for yellow-bellied marmots sunning themselves on large boulders, and listen for the lamb-like bleats of the pika.

Nestled within an alpine meadow, Mistymoon is up a final pitch of 0.8 mile. A couple of campsites are scraped out within the clumps of fir that have been blown into the knotted and twisted contortions known as krummholz. Remember that campfires are not allowed at elevations above 9,200 feet. This restriction includes Mistymoon, Marion, and Helen Lakes.

The drainages around Mistymoon often hold moose during the summer months, including some of the most impressive bulls I've seen in the entire range. As with all wildlife, treat these animals with the utmost respect.

The Mistymoon Trail ends at the southern end of Mistymoon Lake, intersecting with the Solitude Loop Trail (Trail 038). To the east, the trail leads up and over Florence Pass (Hike 8). To the left, the trail wraps around the western edge of Mistymoon, meeting up with the Middle Paint Rock Creek Trail (Trail 066, Hike 13) after 0.6 mile. Lake Solitude lies another 2.5 miles past this junction (Hike 14).

For hikers interested in climbing to the top of Cloud Peak, please reconsider. It's a beast of a hike, full of boulders and lacking in oxygen. It is an amazing view from the top, but it's not an easy hike. And you'll want to be down from the top before afternoon thunderstorms popup. There are no official trails, but you follow the Paint Rock Creek drainage, passing a small waterfall on your way up to the boulders, then rock-hop to the top. The approach basically works around the southeast side of the peak before finishing toward the northwest. You'll want to follow the narrow ridge northwest to the summit. You will feel as though you are circling and false summiting for quite a while. Cairns are sporadic and not all that helpful. Consult *Hiking Wyoming* for an in-depth description of this hike.

Bald Ridge (Trail 097) makes a less crowded hike to Lake Helen. FR 411 is pretty rugged, so you might need to park and walk the road in. Another option is to park at the West Tensleep Trailhead and take Trail 064 west to connect with FR 411 south of Trail 097. Note that the Bald Ridge Cut Off (Trail 064) is not on the National Geographic Cloud Peak Wilderness map. Also keep in mind that there is no wilderness registration box at Trail 097. You need to register at a Forest Service office or at the West Tensleep Trailhead before starting your hike.

Bull moose trio in Mistymoon Lake
TIM FEATHERS

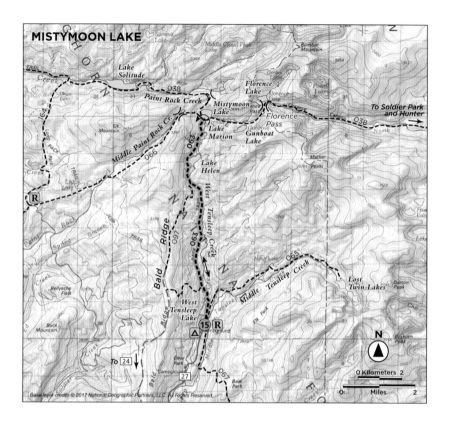

MILES AND DIRECTIONS

0.0   West Tensleep Trailhead.

0.1   Junction with Lost Twin Lakes Trail (Hike 14). Bear left.

1.0   Head of West Tensleep Lake.

1.3   Trail crosses bridge over West Tensleep Creek.

1.4   Junction with Bald Ridge cutoff. Bear right.

4.6   Junction with Bald Ridge Trail. Continue straight ahead.

4.9   Trail reaches foot of Lake Helen.

5.3   Head of Lake Helen.

6.2   Lake Marion.

7.0   Foot of Mistymoon Lake. Junction with trail to Florence Pass.

7.1   Junction with Middle Paint Rock Creek.

7.2   Head of Mistymoon Lake. Lake Solitude Trail climbs away northward.

16. MIDDLE PAINT ROCK CREEK, TRAIL 066

WHY GO?

This is another option for accessing Mistymoon Lake. Compared to the thoroughfare that is the trail from West Tensleep Lake, the Middle Paint Rock Creek Trail is a faint path. The trail follows a scenic drainage, so it is surprising that it doesn't receive heavier foot traffic.

THE RUNDOWN

Distance: 6.2 mile one-way, out-and-back or circuit

Elevation gain: 1,490 feet

Difficulty: Moderate due to distance, elevation, and uneven terrain

Hiking time: About 8 hours

Best seasons: Late spring, summer, fall

Fees and permits: Free Cloud Peak Wilderness Use Registration (available at Battle Park Trailhead)

Trail contacts: Bighorn National Forest, 2013 Eastside 2nd St., Sheridan, WY 82801, (307) 674-2600, http://www.fs.usda.gov/bighorn

Maps: USDA Forest Service Bighorn National Forest, National Geographic Trails Unlimited 720 Cloud Peak Wilderness, USGS Lake Helen, USGS Lake Solitude

Dog-friendly: Dogs must be under control

Trail surface: Uneven terrain

Nearest town: Ten Sleep, Wyoming

Other trail users: ATVs to Lily Lake

Special considerations: The West Tensleep area (including Mistymoon Lake) is subject to restrictions on dispersed camping and regulations that all human waste must be packed out. This is essential to provide positive recreation experiences and protect the natural resources in areas of high use such as this.

FINDING THE TRAILHEAD

 US Hwy. 16 travels by Deer Haven Lodge to the west of Meadowlark Lake. Take FR 27 to the north to go past Deer Haven. After 1.2 miles, veer left onto FR 24, a washboarded but passable road. According to the signs, this is "not an all-weather road," although it is one of the better roads in the forest. FR 24 reaches the Lilly Lake Trailhead after 14+ miles. The Battle Park Trailhead (and wilderness registration box) is a couple of miles beyond this. Watch for oncoming horse trailer traffic on this road, and be prepared to use pullouts to give them room to pass.

Trailhead GPS: N44 18.040' / W107 18.191'

THE HIKE

Before this hike, you'll need to register your entry into Cloud Peak Wilderness. The nearest registration boxes are at Battle Park and West Tensleep Lake Trailheads, or you can register at any of the Forest Service offices.

For the first two miles of this hike, from the parking lot to Lily Lake, Trail 066 is mixed use with ATV users. Here it is a well maintained trail and includes multiple bridge and rock crossing structures to minimize erosion. Lilly Lake is a popular destination for anglers, and it holds a population of Yellowstone cutthroat trout that is occasionally supplemented by a helicopter fish-stocking program.

The 1.8-mile Lily Lake Cutoff Trail (Trail 120) skirts the southern and western ends of Lily Lake before heading northwest, eventually connecting to the Long Park Trail (Trail 164). Long Park Trail runs from the Battle Park Trailhead to Lake Solitude (Hike 14). The Lily Lake Cutoff Trail makes a nice lollipop loop option around Elk Mountain from Battle Park or Lily Lake Trailheads, although it is a bit faint through the wet meadow drainages.

Middle Paint
Rock Creek Trail

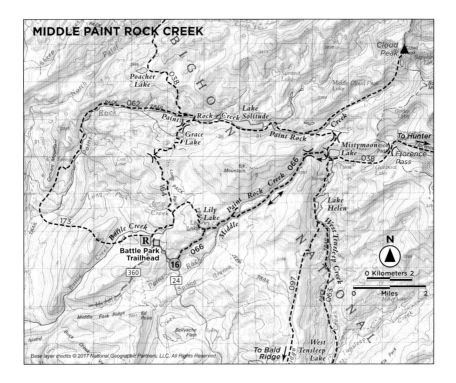

Head east from Lily Lake if continuing on to Mistymoon Lake. From here, the valley views to the southeast are as impressive in their grandness as Elk Mountain is towering above. Elk Mountain is a constant presence along the Middle Paint Rock Creek hike. The trail leads to the divide between this 11,321-foot mountain and the pair of nameless peaks that separate the Middle Paint Rock drainage from the West Tensleep Drainage including Lake Helen, Lake Marion, and the Mistymoon Trail (Hike 15). Cloud Peak stands tall in the background.

Just east of Lily Lake, the nonmotorized use section of Trail 066 continues northeast along the Middle Paint Rock Creek headwaters, while the Bald Ridge ATV Trail 402 heads off to the southeast. Northeast of Lily Lake, the trail crosses a boggy slough before climbing a bit to drier ground along the northern bank of Middle Paint Rock Creek. Shortly, the trail crosses back over this trickle of water, and eventually cruises northeast along the grassy spine of the valley. Ahead, the mountain pass that leads to Mistymoon guides your way. More intense than a leisurely stroll through a mountain meadow, this hike is a long steady climb.

The path crosses into Cloud Peak Wilderness and continues upward. An especially steep incline leads to the krummholz and eventually above timberline to the alpine tundra. After passing a couple of small shallow tarns, the trails cut east along the southern banks of another of these nameless high-elevation glacial ponds. Cresting the final divide, Cloud Peak and Bomber Mountain dominate the view, both towering over Mistymoon Lake. Trail 066 intersects the Solitude Loop Trail (Trail 038) just north of Mistymoon. A left takes you into the Paint Rock Creek Basin and to Lake Solitude. A right turn travels along the western edge of Mistymoon Lake, intersecting the Mistymoon Trail (Trail 063) in about 0.6 mile.

MILES AND DIRECTIONS

0.0   Lily Lake Trailhead.

2.0   Lily Lake.

3.9   Trail enters Cloud Peak Wilderness.

6.2   Trail junction at Mistymoon Lake.

17. LAKE SOLITUDE TRAIL, TRAILS 164 & 038

WHY GO?

A well-worn network of trails leads the way to Lake Solitude, a gateway to the entire Cloud Peak Wilderness and the largest natural lake in the Bighorns. This route is popular with horse packers departing from the Battle Park Trailhead.

THE RUNDOWN

Distance: 6.2 miles one-way to Lake Solitude, 10.1 miles one-way to Mistymoon Lake, out-and-back or circuit

Elevation gain: 2,100 feet

Difficulty: Moderate due to distance

Hiking time: About 8 hours

Best seasons: Late spring, summer, early fall

Fees and permits: Free Cloud Peak Wilderness Use Registration

Trail contacts: Bighorn National Forest, 2013 Eastside 2nd St., Sheridan, WY 82801, (307)

674-2600, http://www.fs.usda.gov/bighorn

Maps: USDA Forest Service Bighorn National Forest, National Geographic Trails Unlimited 720 Cloud Peak Wilderness, USGS Lake Solitude, USGS Lake Helen

Dog-friendly: Dogs must be under control

Trail surface: Uneven terrain, heavily rutted in places

Nearest town: Ten Sleep, Wyoming

Other trail users: Equestrians

Special considerations: None

FINDING THE TRAILHEAD

US Hwy. 16 travels by Deer Haven Lodge to the west of Meadowlark Lake. Take FR 27 to the north to go past Deer Haven. After 1.2 miles, veer left onto FR 24 a washboarded but passable road. According to the signs, this is "not an all-weather road," although it is one of the better roads in the forest. FR 24 reaches Battle Park Trailhead after 16.3 miles. Hikers can park in the upper parking lot beyond the wilderness registration box. Watch for oncoming horse trailer traffic on this road, and be prepared to use pullouts to give them room to pass.

Trailhead GPS: N44 18.528' / W107 18.747'

THE HIKE

A popular route into the Cloud Peak Wilderness from Battle Park Trailhead, this hike (Trails 164 and 038) goes through some timber, then along the broad meadow of Long Park, before working around the flanks of Elk Mountain.

The trail continues north until Cloud Peak emerges in the distance from behind the slopes of Elk Mountain. Expect to share Long Park with grazing cattle during the summer grazing. Trail posts are good scratching posts for cows, so a wagon wheel of animal trail spokes fan out from these hubs. This makes the posts a bit confusing as reference points in some instances. You can line up the trail posts and get a general idea of where Trail 120 heads off to Lily Lake.

Beyond the northern end of the 1.6-mile Long Park, the route turns northeast and crosses through timbered lands and pocket meadows. It follows the base of a steep boulder field before the network of trails crisscross a marshy basin. Bearing right, the trail descends eastward through spruce and fir, eventually meandering back westward to wrap around the western shore of Grace Lake. Past the lake, the

Elk Mountain and Long Park

Elk Mountain from Lake
Solitude Trail

trail enters the Cloud Peak Wilderness, and 4.7 miles from the trailhead, it intersects the Solitude Loop Trail (Trail 038).

The main trail runs east-west along Paint Rock Creek from this intersection,
and 0.3 mile to the west, the Solitude Loop Trail heads north to Poacher Lake
(Hike 18), while Trail 062 continues west 3.1 miles to the wilderness boundary,
and then runs south 1.5 miles as an ATV trail to the Hyatt Cow Camp. To the east,
the trail takes you to the foot of Lake Solitude in 1.2 miles and to the head of the
lake a mile beyond.

From Lake Solitude, one can continue to Mistymoon Lake or peel off the main
trail and follow the Paint Rock Creek drainage up in an attempt to summit Cloud
Peak (see Hike 15 and *Hiking Wyoming* for more information).

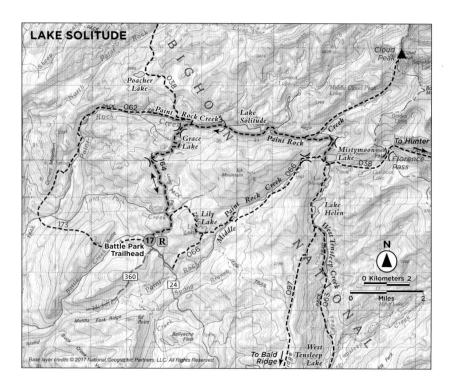

MILES AND DIRECTIONS

0.0   Battle Park Trailhead.

0.2   Trail crosses head of Battle Creek.

0.8   Trail enters Long Park.

1.2   Trail crosses Long Park Creek.

2.4   Trail leaves Long Park.

4.3   Grace Lake.

4.7   Trail enters Cloud Peak Wilderness.

5.0   Junction with Paint Rock Trail. Turn right.

6.2   Trail reaches foot of Lake Solitude.

7.1   Trail reaches head of Lake Solitude and fords inlet.

7.5   Waterfalls.

8.5   Trail fords Paint Rock Creek.

9.5   Trail crosses pass into West Tensleep drainage.

10.1 Head of Mistymoon Lake. Mistymoon Lake Trail follows western shore of the lake.

18. **POACHER LAKE, TRAIL 038**

WHY GO?

The Poacher Lake Trail is the western segment of the Solitude Loop Trail (Trail 038) that rings the Cloud Peak Wilderness. Poacher Lake lies between Trail 059 (access from Lower Paint Rock Lake Trailhead) and Trail 062 (access from Hyatt Cow Camp, Battle Park Trailhead, or West Tensleep Lake Trailhead).

THE RUNDOWN

Distance: 3.7 miles connecting trail

Elevation gain: 810 feet

Difficulty: Moderate due to uneven footing, distance from trailheads

Hiking time: About 2 hours

Best seasons: Summer, early fall

Fees and permits: Free Cloud Peak Wilderness Use Registration

Trail contacts: Bighorn National Forest, 2013 Eastside 2nd St., Sheridan, WY 82801, (307)

674-2600, http://www.fs.usda.gov/bighorn

Maps: USDA Forest Service Bighorn National Forest, National Geographic Trails Unlimited 720 Cloud Peak Wilderness, USGS Lake Solitude, USGS Shell Lake

Dog-friendly: Dogs must be under control

Trail surface: Uneven terrain

Nearest town: Ten Sleep, Wyoming

Other trail users: Equestrians

FINDING THE TRAILHEAD

 The Poacher Lake Trail is a segment of the Solitude Loop Trail (Trail 038). It is an extension from the Lake Solitude route (Hike 17) and connects with Geneva Pass (Hike 21).

Trailhead GPS: N44 21.439' / W107 17.632'

THE HIKE

This trail is the southwestern link of the Solitude Loop Trail (Trail 038), but Poacher Lake makes a great destination in its own right. Poacher Lake is 5.9 miles from the Lower Paint Rock Lake Trailhead (Hike 19), about 7 miles from Hyatt Cow Camp (along Trail 062), about 8 miles from Battle Park Trailhead (Hike 17), or about 14.5 miles from the West Tensleep Lake Trailhead (Hike 15). No matter where you start this hike, be sure to obtain your free Cloud Peak Wilderness Registration before you begin.

This 3.7-mile trail runs from the main fork of Paint Rock Creek in the south to the North Paint Rock Creek. From Paint Rock Creek, north of Grace Lake and west of Lake Solitude, the trail climbs westward up the bluffs to the north of Paint Rock Creek. As it switchbacks up along the bases of granite outcrops, the views of Elk Mountain to the southeast are unobstructed. Beyond this, the climb continues, and the canopy of lodgepole pine closes in. After about a mile, the hike crests, dropping down and leveling off. Here, along the cooler north-facing slope, the forest shifts to spruce and fir. Beyond this, it levels off along a marshy basin. The wet meadow runs to the east, but after crossing the stream, the trail heads west three quarters of a mile to intersect Poacher Lake.

Poacher is a broad and shallow pond, and the meadows surrounding it are full of wildlife signs. Look for elk scat, somewhat round in shape with a dimple on one end and a pimple on the other. Moose scat is more oval in shape and might also be found.

From Poacher, the trail continues for a mile and a half, initially up an incline, before descending to Teepee Pole Flats and North Paint Rock Creek. After a

Bull moose in the fall
CHARLES HUBBELL

crossing, the trail reaches the intersection with Trail 059 (see Hike 19). The Solitude Loop Trail (Trail 038) continues over Geneva Pass from here (see Hike 21).

A healthy population of cutthroat trout lives in Poacher Lake, and the Wyoming Game & Fish Department occasionally supplement this with helicopter releases of fingerling trout.

Elephant Head

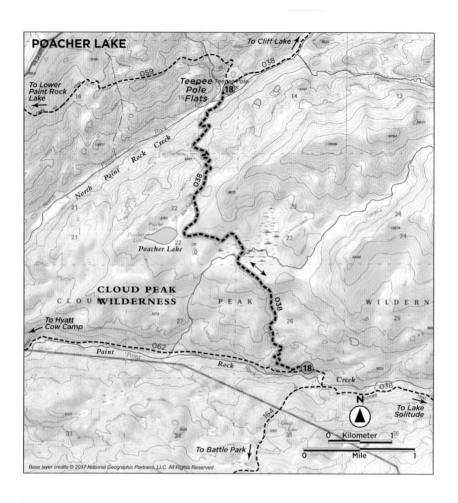

MILES AND DIRECTIONS

0.0 Trail leaves Paint Rock Trail.

0.5 Trail crosses small stream.

1.5 Trail crosses marshy brook.

2.3 Poacher Lake.

3.8 Trail fords North Paint Rock Creek to reach the junction with Cliff Lake Trail (Hike 19).

19. CLIFF LAKE, TRAILS 059, 038, & 060

WHY GO?

The Cliff Lake route intersects the Solitude Loop Trail (Trail 038) at Teepee Pole Flats, a scenic opening with good views of the peaks. From here hikers follow North Paint Rock Creek for 2.6 miles. At this intersection, hikers can continue along the creek and over Geneva Pass or take the side trip loop to explore a collection of stunning glacial lakes, including Cliff Lake as well as neighboring Crater Lakes, Lake Eunice, and Sheepherder Lake.

THE RUNDOWN

Distance: 11.6 miles one-way, out-and-back or circuit

Elevation gain: 2,275 feet

Difficulty: Moderate due to elevation gains and uneven terrain

Hiking time: About 5 hours

Best seasons: Summer, early fall

Fees and permits: Free Cloud Peak Wilderness Use Registration

Trail contacts: Bighorn National Forest, 2013 Eastside 2nd St., Sheridan, WY 82801, (307)

674-2600, http://www.fs.usda.gov/bighorn

Maps: USDA Forest Service Bighorn National Forest, National Geographic Trails Unlimited 720 Cloud Peak Wilderness, USGS Spanish Point, USGS Cloud Peak, USGS Shell Lake

Dog-friendly: Dogs must be under control

Trail surface: Uneven terrain

Nearest town: Ten Sleep, Wyoming

Other trail users: ATVs until the wilderness boundary

FINDING THE TRAILHEAD

Look for FR 17 off of US Hwy. 14 between Shell Falls and Granite Pass. Turn onto FR 17 and follow this rough road east and then south for 25.5 miles to reach the Lower Paint Rock Trailhead. Alternatively, the northern stretches of this trail can be a connection between the Poacher Lake Hike (Hike 18) and the Geneva Pass Hike (Hike 21).

Trailhead GPS: N44 23.729' / W107 22.865'

THE HIKE

This hike shares the trail with ATVs for the first 1.7 miles from Lower Paint Rock Lake Trailhead to just beyond the Sheep Creek crossing. Hiking south from the trailhead, keep left at the split of Trails 059 and 116 (the Kinky White Trail). The path (Trail 059) heads into the timber starting with a steady uphill climb. Beyond Sheep Creek, the trail enters the Cloud Peak Wilderness.

The next 2 miles are a series of ups and downs, all the while maintaining an elevation of around 9,500 feet. The forest reveals an occasional wet meadow before the trail drops down into the opening of Teepee Pole Flats along North Paint Rock Creek.

Approaching the 5-mile mark, Trail 059 ends as it picks up the Solitude Loop Trail (Trail 038). To the right are Poacher Lake (Hike 18), Lake Solitude (Hike 17), and destinations beyond. Take a left to follow the meadow upstream. The trail continues its northeast trajectory, gaining elevation with nearly every step.

The mountains reveal themselves at the junction with the Geneva Pass Trail (Hike 21). Trail 038, the left trail, continues north along North Paint Rock Creek and leads directly to Geneva Pass. Trail 060 is a 4-mile horseshoe trail that comes out on Trail 038 just 1.6 miles north of this junction. This side detour hikes past Cliff Lake and Lake Eunice and provides access to boulder-hopping destinations, including the Crater Lakes, Sheepherder Lake, and Rainbow Lake.

Keep right at the Geneva Pass Trail junction to follow Trail 060 along a rushing tributary stream. After a stiff climb through a stand of subalpine fir, the trail emerges amid a series of grassy balds. It winds upward, following the pretty mountain brook that drains Cliff Lake. The first pool at the foot of the cliffs is a shallow, narrow pond. Cliff Lake lies beyond it, bordered to the north by subalpine forest and to the south by a sheer wall of granite rising 700 feet above the water. The best views are from the head of the lake, where the trail climbs onto meadow hillocks above the wetlands at the east end.

The trail then continues upward along the stream, passing a slender waterfall that descends across the rounded face to the south. The route now leads onto open moors where the trees are scarce and rocky knobs rise from the rolling tundra. Soon the broad mirror of Lake Elsa can be seen, and before long, the path reaches the shore of Lake Eunice.

From Lake Eunice, the trail climbs hills of granite in a more westerly direction as the trail turns back toward the Solitude Loop Trail. Looking back, you'll be able to see Black Tooth Mountain looming over the glacial carved divide you're hiking away from.

Ultimately, you drop back down to North Paint Rock Creek. Crossing the creek, you end up back on Trail 038, just 1.6 miles north of where you departed the trail. Robin Lake and then Geneva Pass are to the north of this intersection.

Pika

MILES AND DIRECTIONS

0.0 Lower Paint Rock Trailhead.

0.2 Junction with Kinky White Trail. Turn left.

1.9 Trail crosses Sheep Creek.

2.3 Cloud Peak Wilderness.

4.9 Teepee Pole Flats.

6.9 Trail fords North Paint Rock Creek.

7.5 Junction with end of Geneva Pass Trail (Hike 21). Bear right.

8.3 Trail fords outlet of Cliff Lake.

9.7 Lake Eunice. Junction with route to Rainbow Lake. Bear left.

11.5 Trail fords headwaters of North Paint Rock Creek.

11.6 Junction with Geneva Pass Trail.

POWDER RIVER PASS AND WESTERN WILDERNESS ACCESS ADDITIONAL HIKES

Willow Park Nordic Ski Trail (Trail 556) is 13 miles of groomed winter-sports trails. This network of loop options for summertime exploring is found near Meadowlark Lake.

High Line Trail (Trail 67) connects Deer Park Campground to East Tensleep Lake. It makes a great loop when coupled with the **Tensleep Trail** (Trail 156, Hike 12) and the **East Tensleep Trail** (Trail 068).

The Pasture Park Trail (Trail 410) explores the lands southwest of the James T. Saban Lookout (Trail 070, Hike 10). You can create a pleasant lollipop hike by combining this trail with a short section of FR 436, the **Leigh Creek Crossing Trail** (Trail 413), and the **Leigh Cabin Trail** (Trail 412).

NORTHERN WILDERNESS ACCESS

Coffeen Park Trailhead offers up many routes to hike the northern reaches of the Cloud Peak Wilderness. It's reached via a maze of slow traveling high clearance roads that become impassable in inclement weather. This keeps foot traffic down when compared to the trails in the southern end of the wilderness area. Edelman and Geneva Passes cross the spine of the Bighorns. You can head east along the Solitude Loop Trail from here as well.

An extensive network of ATV trails is found in The Reservoirs section, and the Solitude Loop Trail follows these for a bit in areas outside of the Cloud Peak Wilderness. The views are impressive here.

The expansive Rock Creek Roadless Area is adjacent to the Cloud Peak Wilderness. Hikers and horseback riders use Bud Love Wildlife Management Area and the HF–Bar Ranch as jumping off points to the Rock Creek Watershed. One can intersect the Solitude Loop Trail near Elk Lake from these trails. Some trails in these parts receive minimal maintenance, and this can provide options for explorers looking to get off the beaten path.

Cloud Peak Wilderness sign

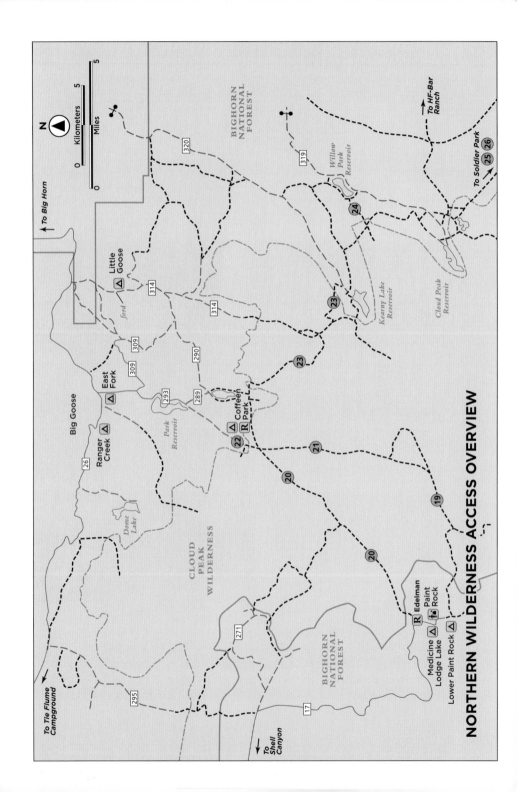

NORTHERN WILDERNESS ACCESS OVERVIEW

20. EDELMAN PASS, TRAIL 025

WHY GO?

This gorgeous trail can be approached as a thru-hike connecting the Edelman Pass Trailhead to Coffeen Park, or it can be coupled with Geneva Pass to create an impressive loop hitting many of the highlights of the northern Cloud Peak Wilderness.

THE RUNDOWN

Distance: 22 miles round trip out-and-back, 11 miles point-to-point, can also be a circuit

Elevation gain: 2,020 feet

Difficulty: Strenuous due to distance, elevation, and uneven terrain

Hiking time: About 15 hours

Best seasons: Early summer, fall

Fees and permits: Free Cloud Peak Wilderness Use Registration

Trail contacts: Bighorn National Forest, 2013 Eastside 2nd St., Sheridan, WY 82801, (307)

674-2600, http://www.fs.usda.gov/bighorn

Maps: USDA Forest Service Bighorn National Forest, National Geographic Trails Unlimited 720 Cloud Peak Wilderness, USGS Park Reservoir, USGS Dome Lake, USGS Shell Lake, USGS Spanish Point

Dog-friendly: Dogs must be under control

Trail surface: Uneven terrain

Nearest town: Shell, Manderson, or Ten Sleep, Wyoming

Other trail users: Motorcycles until wilderness boundary

FINDING THE TRAILHEAD

Look for FR 17 off of US Hwy. 14 between Shell Falls and Granite Pass. Turn onto FR 17 and follow this rough road east and then south for nearly 25 miles to reach the trailhead just north of the Medicine Lodge Lakes and the Lower Paint Rock Trailhead.

Trailhead GPS: N44 24.801' / W107 22.964'

THE HIKE

With lush meadows, high-elevation lakes, alpine tundra, and a mountain pass, the Edelman Pass Trail is representative of the Bighorn Mountains experience.

After the Edelman Pass Trail (Trail 25) leaves FR 17, expect a small spring creek crossing. From here, the hike enters the Cloud Peak Wilderness (self-registration permits were required at the trailhead). Note that motorcycles are allowed on this first 0.5-mile stretch of trail before it enters the wilderness.

The hiking initially is along a broad meadow as you parallel Medicine Lodge Creek. After 2.6 miles, you'll ford the creek at the head of this meadow. From here, the elevation continues to climb. The hike enters a more forested landscape for a bit before pushing above treeline as you near Emerald Lake.

Crossing over a nameless pass, Emerald Lake reveals itself below. The lake receives periodic stocking of Yellowstone cutthroat trout fingerlings, and the fishing can be hot here.

Trail 032 heads off to the northwest from here, passing the string of lakes collectively known as the Lakes of the Rough and Shell Lake before ending along FR 280. (Note the National Geographic Map has a mistake on Trail 032. The trail actually passes to the south of the 2nd Lake of the Rough.)

Yellow-bellied Marmot
TIM FEATHERS

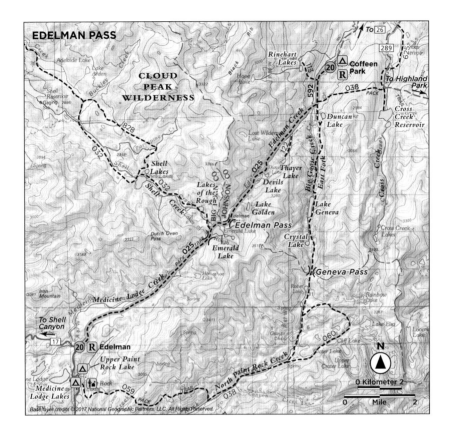

The Edelman Pass trail continues northeast from Emerald Lake. You cross Edelman Pass to enter the Edelman Creek watershed. The first couple of miles down from the pass are steep and rocky. Winter can linger long here on these talus slopes. Good thing the pika that live here store up haystacks of grasses to help them survive the cold season.

Shortly after the trail crosses Edelman Creek, a 0.1-mile spur trail (Trail 123) leads east to Devils Lake. This makes a nice spot to ditch the backpack for a few minutes. Anglers can thrash the waters for eager brook trout.

Beyond this spur, the trail continues downhill for another mile or so. Look for historic cabin ruins, the site of early mining claims near where Trail 122 heads to Thayer Lake. Thayer Lake holds brook trout as well as some lake trout, including a few sizable ones.

From the Thayer Lake Trail junction, the Edelman Trail heads in a straight-shot for 1.2 miles to hit the Geneva Pass Trail. You'll make two stream crossings on the way to this junction. First, it's Edelman Creek, followed by the East Fork of Big Goose Creek.

Right after this crossing, you hit Trail 038 less than a mile south of the Coffeen Park Trailhead. If you're headed to Coffeen Park, you'll turn left to head north. Trail 038 will soon head off to the east toward Cross Creek Reservoir and eventually Lake Winnie (see Hike 23). You'll continue north on Trail 592 to reach Coffeen Park. If you're aiming for Geneva Pass (see Hike 21), you'll head south (right) and continue onward.

MILES AND DIRECTIONS

0.0   Trail leaves FR 17.

0.3   Trail crosses small spring creek.

0.5   Trail enters Cloud Peak Wilderness.

2.6   Trail fords Medicine Lodge Creek.

5.0   Trail crosses pass to enter Shell Creek drainage.

5.7   Edelman Pass. Trail starts descending.

6.7   Trail crosses Edelman Creek and follows west bank.

7.5   Trail crosses to east bank of Edelman Creek.

7.6   Junction with trail to Devils Lake (0.2 mile, easy). Bear left for Coffeen Park.

7.7   Trail returns to west bank of Edelman Creek.

8.7   Ruins of old mine.

8.8   Junction with abandoned trail to Thayer Lake. Continue straight ahead.

9.6   Trail makes final ford of Edelman Creek.

9.8   Trail fords East Fork of Big Goose Creek.

9.9   Junction with Geneva Pass Trail (Hike 21). Bear left for Coffeen Park.

11.0   Coffeen Park Trailhead.

21. GENEVA PASS, TRAILS 592 & 038

WHY GO?

The Geneva Pass Trail (the western section of the Solitude Loop Trail) heads straight south from Coffeen Park Trailhead, continuing along the East Fork of Big Goose Creek. It provides multiple good options for backpacking as it passes Lake Geneva and Crystal Lake. It continues over Geneva Pass before descending down along North Paint Rock Creek.

THE RUNDOWN

Distance: 8.4 miles one-way, out-and-back or circuit

Elevation gain: 1,775 feet

Difficulty: Strenuous due to length, elevation, stream crossings, and uneven footing

Hiking time: About 11 hours round trip

Best seasons: Summer, fall

Fees and permits: Free Cloud Peak Wilderness Use Registration

Trail contacts: Bighorn National Forest, 2013 Eastside 2nd St., Sheridan, WY 82801, (307)

674-2600, http://www.fs.usda.gov/bighorn

Maps: USDA Forest Service Bighorn National Forest, National Geographic Trails Unlimited 720 Cloud Peak Wilderness, USGS Park Reservoir, USGS Cloud Peak, USGS, Shell Lake, USGS Dome Lake

Dog-friendly: Dogs must be under control

Trail surface: Uneven terrain

Nearest town: Big Horn, Wyoming

Other trail users: Equestrians

Special considerations: None

FINDING THE TRAILHEAD

It is a long and bumpy ride to the Coffeen Park Trailhead. High clearance and four-wheel drive is recommended. Take Red Grade Road/FR 26 (either from US Hwy. 14 or from Big Horn), to just east of the Big Goose Ranger Station. Turn south onto FR 293. This is a primitive but passable road. Travel 5.1 miles to reach the Spear-O-Wigwam Lodge, traveling along the eastern end of Park Reservoir along the way. The road gets progressively worse for the final 3.1 miles. Past the lodge, bear right to keep on FR 293. You'll pass Cross Creek Campground. Consider parking here and hiking the final stretch of road. **Trailhead GPS:** N44 31.128' / W107 14.721'

THE HIKE

Getting to the Coffeen Park Trailhead is a long and slow process involving narrow bumpy roads, serious ruts, and a couple of stream crossings. High clearance is essential, and four-wheel drive is encouraged. Like all primitive roads in the Bighorns, traveling on wet roads is ill advised. It's not worth damaging the roads.

After reaching the Coffeen Park Trailhead, it will feel good to stretch those legs out a bit. Cloud Peak Wilderness registration is required for this hike, and a self-registration box is at the start of the trail.

This hike basically follows the East Fork of Big Goose Creek up to the headwaters above Crystal Lake near Geneva Pass some 5.8 miles ahead. Not far from the trailhead, you'll see the creek crossing that leads to Rinehart Lakes (Hike 22) off to the west. Trail 592 quickly crosses the Cloud Peak Wilderness boundary and merges with the Solitude Loop Trail (Trail 038). To the east along Trail 038 is the Highland Park and Lake Winnie segment (Hike 23) of the Solitude Loop.

Continue south (straight) for the Geneva Pass Trail. Two tenths of a mile beyond, the Edelman Pass Trail (Hike 20) splits off to the southwest (right) from the Geneva Pass Trail. Again, you want to continue straight ahead. After another 0.5 mile, another side trail materializes. To the left, Trail 125 is a short spur to Duncan Lake, a shallow quite pool of a pond.

Views are fairly limited on this stretch of the Geneva Pass Trail. A few rocky talus slopes provide an occasional gap in the tree cover. Long abandoned log cabin ruins from the gold prospecting days of the 1920s remain visible as the hike continues on.

Nearly 2.5 miles into the hike, the trail crosses the East Fork of Big Goose Creek and follows the western banks for a mile, pressing upwards, eventually crossing back over to the eastern bank of the creek and reaching Lake Geneva. The long, skinny lake tucks in nicely at the base steep slopes. The trail runs along the eastern end of Lake Geneva under the cover of trees. Lake Geneva is a doable day trip, but because the slow traveling access road eats up so much time, it's often preferred to campout for at least a night.

From here, head steeply up the ridge toward Crystal Lake, situated at the base of a towering granite face. The final push through alpine meadows and talus boulder fields brings you up and over 10,275-foot Geneva Pass.

South of Geneva Pass, Robin Lake marks the headwaters of the North Paint Rock Creek. Beyond Robin Lake, the pass remains narrow. The trail rock-hops between a pair of nameless ponds before reaching the northern intersection of the Cliff Lake spur (Trail 060, Hike 19). This 4-mile side-trip visits alpine gems including Lake Eunice and Cliff Lake, before reuniting with Trail 038. If you bypass the Cliff Lake spur, Trail 038 continues south 1.6 miles. After a pair of stream crossings, you'll reach the southern intersection of these two trails.

East Fork Big
Goose Creek

Beyond this, the Solitude Loop Trail (Trail 038) continues on to Poacher Lake (Hike 18) and Lake Solitude (Hike 17). Another option is to head west at Teepee Pole Flats on Trail 059 (Hike 19). Many hikers opt to take this trail and loop back to Coffeen Park via Edelman Pass (see Hike 20).

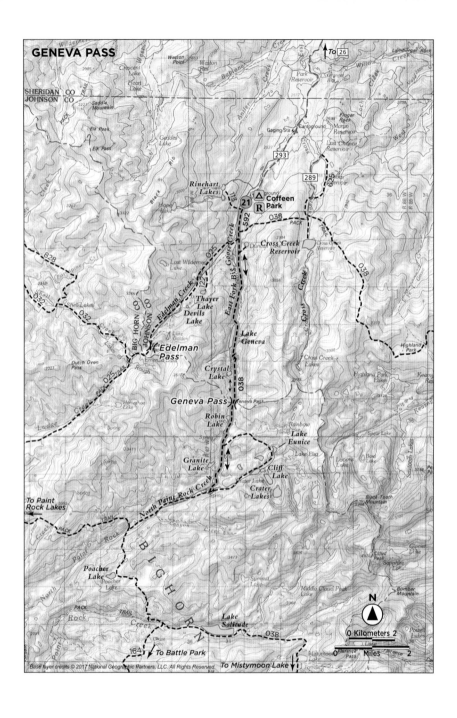

Coffeen Park Trailhead

MILES AND DIRECTIONS

0.0   Coffeen Park Trailhead.

0.2   Junction with Rinehart Lakes Trail. Continue straight ahead.

0.9   Junction with cutoff trail from Cross Creek. Continue straight.

1.1   Junction with Edelman Pass Trail. Bear left.

1.6   Junction with trail to Duncan Lake (0.4 mile, easy). Continue straight ahead for Lake Geneva and Geneva Pass.

2.4   Trail fords East Fork of Big Goose Creek and follows west bank.

3.4   Foot of Lake Geneva. Trial fords the outlet.

4.1   Trail leaves head of Lake Geneva.

4.8   Junction with trail to Crystal Lake (0.1 mile, easy). Continue straight.

5.8   Geneva pass. Trail descends into North Paint Rock drainage.

6.2   Robin Lake.

6.7   Trail fords North Paint Rock Creek.

6.8   Signpost marks end of Cliff Lake Trail. Continue straight ahead.

7.5   Gap to the west leads to Granite Lake.

8.0   Trail fords North Paint Rock Creek.

8.3   Trail fords outlet stream of Cliff Lake.

8.4   Trail ends at junction with Cliff Lake Trail.

22. **RINEHART LAKES, TRAILS 592 & 113**

WHY GO?

This is a short but steep burst hiking from Coffeen Park Trailhead, crossing the East Fork of Big Goose Creek, and climbing up to Rinehart (also spelled Rhinehart) Lakes. Both lakes are fishable, and they make for a nice side trip if you are in the area.

THE RUNDOWN

Distance: 1.4 miles out-and-back

Elevation gain: 500 feet

Difficulty: Moderate due to elevation gains, uneven footing, and stream crossing

Hiking time: About 1 hour

Best seasons: Summer, fall

Fees and permits: Free Cloud Peak Wilderness Use Registration

Trail contacts: Bighorn National Forest, 2013 Eastside 2nd St., Sheridan, WY 82801, (307)

674-2600, http://www.fs.usda.gov/bighorn

Maps: USDA Forest Service Bighorn National Forest, National Geographic Trails Unlimited 720 Cloud Peak Wilderness, USGS Dome Lake, USGS Park Reservoir

Dog-friendly: Dogs must be under control

Trail surface: Uneven terrain

Nearest town: Big Horn, Wyoming

Other trail users: None

FINDING THE TRAILHEAD

It is a long and bumpy ride to the Coffeen Park Trailhead. High clearance and four-wheel drive are recommended. Take Red Grade Road/FR 26 (either from US Hwy. 14 or from Big Horn), to just east of the Big Goose Ranger Station. Turn south onto FR 293. This is a primitive but passable road. Travel 5.1 miles to reach the Spear-O-Wigwam Lodge, traveling along the eastern end of Park Reservoir along the way. The road gets progressively worse for the final 3.1 miles. Past the lodge, bear right to keep on FR 293. You'll pass Cross Creek Campground. Consider parking here and hiking the final stretch of road. **Trailhead GPS:** N44 31.128' / W107 14.721'

THE HIKE

Be sure to register at the trailhead as this hike enters the Cloud Peak Wilderness. From the Coffeen Park Trailhead, go south 0.2 mile on Trail 592. Take a right at the wide track that leads down to the East Fork of Big Goose Creek. The water crossing will feel refreshing as the next half a mile is straight up the side of the mountain. Lodgepole pine canopy keeps you shaded as you climb 500 feet. Eventually you pop over the ridge and find yourself at Upper Rinehart Lake. Pick yourself a boulder perch to fish from or continue north through the woods to Lower Rinehart Lake.

Big Goose Creek crossing

Rinehart Lakes

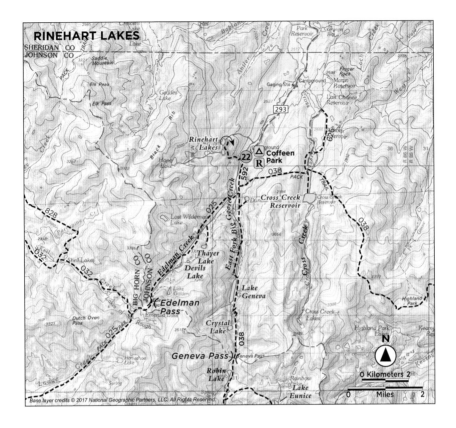

Like many mountain lakes in the Bighorn Mountains, Wyoming Game & Fish stock these waters with trout on a rotating schedule. Recent sampling documented rainbow trout between 6 and 16 inches.

This is a popular day trip for people camping in the area, but the remote nature of the Coffeen Park Trailhead helps keep fishing pressure moderate.

MILES AND DIRECTIONS

- **0.0** Coffeen Park Trailhead. Follow Geneva Pass Trail south.
- **0.2** Junction with Rinehart Lakes Trail. Turn right and ford East Fork of Big Goose Creek.
- **0.3** Trail enters Cloud Peak Wilderness.
- **0.7** Rinehart Lakes.

23. HIGHLAND PARK AND LAKE WINNIE, TRAILS 038, 036, & 014

WHY GO?

A long segment of the Solitude Loop Trail (Trail 038), this stretch travels through stunning Highland Park as it connects Coffeen Park Trailhead to Lake Winnie. Highland Park offers amazing views of the high mountain peaks including Black Tooth Mountain.

THE RUNDOWN

Distance: 14.1 miles long handled lollipop 8.4 miles one-way Coffeen Park to Highland Park, 5.7 miles Lake Winnie Loop

Elevation gain: 1,900 feet

Difficulty: Strenuous due to distance, elevation gains, and uneven footing

Hiking time: About 7 hours

Best seasons: Summer, early fall

Fees and permits: Free Cloud Peak Wilderness Use Registration

Trail contacts: Bighorn National Forest, 2013 Eastside 2nd

St., Sheridan, WY 82801, (307) 674-2600, http://www.fs.usda.gov/bighorn

Maps: USDA Forest Service Bighorn National Forest, National Geographic Trails Unlimited 720 Cloud Peak Wilderness, USGS Park Reservoir, USGS Cloud Peak, USGS Willow Park Reservoir

Dog-friendly: Dogs must be under control

Trail surface: Uneven terrain

Nearest town: Big Horn, Wyoming

Other trail users: Equestrians

FINDING THE TRAILHEAD

It is a long and bumpy ride to the Coffeen Park Trailhead. High clearance and four-wheel drive is recommended. Take Red Grade Road/FR 26 (either from US Hwy. 14 or from Big Horn), to just east of the Big Goose Ranger Station. Turn south onto FR 293. This is a primitive but passable road. Travel 5.1 miles to reach the Spear-O-Wigwam Lodge, traveling along the eastern end of Park Reservoir along the way. The road gets progressively worse for the final 3.1 miles. Past the lodge, bear right to keep on FR 293. You'll pass Cross Creek Campground. Consider parking here and hiking the final stretch of road. **Trailhead GPS:** N44 31.128' / W107 14.721'

THE HIKE

This hike represents the northeast arm of the Cloud Peak Wilderness. It is an essential connection in the Solitude Loop Trail (Trail 038), but can also be a destination for day hikes and overnight trips. Primitive access roads are a limiting factor here.

Register at the Coffeen Park Trailhead. Trail 592 goes from the parking area, past the Rinehart Lakes Trail (Hike 22) and connects to Trail 038 just over half a mile from the trailhead. The Geneva Pass Trail (Hike 21) continues south from here, while this hike heads left (roughly east).

A 2.2-mile stretch offers up a steady climb through the shaded forests. It flattens out before descending to Cross Creek. The Cloud Peak Wilderness boundary doglegs to exclude Cross Creek Reservoir and the motorized route that leads to it. At this intersection, a left and then quick right will keep you on Trail 038 and the Highland Park and Lake Winnie segment of the Solitude Loop Trail. After crossing Cross Creek, the trail reenters the wilderness area.

Another climb under the canopy of forest cover is in store, and eventually the trail flirts with timberline. Views of the peaks are distracting, in the best possible way. Stubby little alpine plants grow in short cushions, eking out an existence in a harsh environment. Wind whipped and contorted, subalpine fir trees grow in scattered stands of krummholz. Trail 027 comes in from the north, and then a steep and rocky descent leads into the East Fork of Little Goose Creek's headwaters basin. The path crosses this trickle of water.

The trail then climbs another ridge before dropping out through the square mile of open meadows that make up Highland Park. Wildlife utilizes Highland Park, which is a mosaic of boggy wet meadows and drier upland fields dominated by blossoms of lupine, forget-me-not, and buttercup. Views of Black Tooth Mountain dominate the skyline to the south.

The trail splits near the southeast corner of Highland Park. For backpackers setting up camp here, multiple day trip options exist. One choice is making a 6+ mile loop to Lake Winnie and Kearny Lake Reservoir. A 7+ mile out-and-back option would be the trip to Highland Lake, a nice waterfall, and beyond to Spear Lake.

For this hike (and the Solitude Loop), the trail continues from the southeast corner of Highland Park, heading onward to Lake Winnie. After crossing a broad saddle to the east, the trail continues northeast along rocky talus slopes. Winter snowdrifts linger late into summer here, while alpine wildflowers sprinkle dazzling colors like confetti on the landscape. The trail makes a broad U-turn at the head of the basin above Lake Winnie, coursing roughly southeast through the open woodlands toward an unnamed lake and then Lake Winnie. Enjoy views of jagged Black Tooth Mountain and conical Penrose Peak from the lake.

The trail runs east from here, exiting the Cloud Peak Wilderness. The path crosses a boggy wet meadow and wanders amid damp spruce flats, before reaching a trail junction. Heading west, Trail 036 keeps on the northern side of Kearny Lake Reservoir as it leads to Highland Lake and eventually Spear Lake. Another option is to take Trail 036 for 1.9 miles, then merge onto Trail 414, a path of switchbacks that leads 1.2 miles back to Highland Park, closing the Lake Winnie Loop.

Silvery lupine is common throughout the Bighorn Mountains
MOLLY MCKAY

This intersection also marks incoming ATV Trail 320, which connects Penrose Park to the northeast with Kearny Lake. Hikers share the trail with ATVs for 0.3 mile on the final approach to Kearny Lake.

From Kearny Lake, The Reservoirs (Hike 24) is a mixed-use trail that serves as a connecting trail for the Solitude Loop Trail.

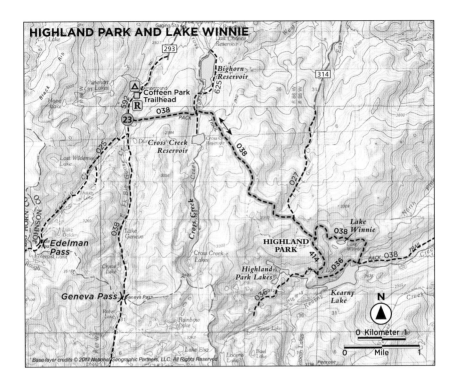

MILES AND DIRECTIONS

0.0 Coffeen Park Trailhead.

0.2 Junction with Rinehart Lakes Trail. Continue straight.

0.6 Junction with Solitude Loop (Trail 038). Head east (left).

2.8 Cross Creek.

6.6 Junction with Trail 027 from the north. Continue ahead.

8.4 Highland Park. Start of 5.7-mile Lake Winnie Loop.

9.7 Lake Winnie.

11.0 Intersection with Trails 320, 036, and 038 (Hike 24). Take 036 right (to the west) for the Lake Winnie Loop.

12.9 Trail junction. Trail 036 goes left to Highland Lake and Spear Lake. Trail 414 goes right to complete Lake Winnie Loop and return to Highland Park.

14.1 Return to Highland Park.

24. THE RESERVOIRS, TRAIL 038

WHY GO?

While much of the official Solitude Loop Trail (Trail 038) is within the boundaries of the Cloud Peak Wilderness, the stretch of trail between Lake Winnie and Elk Lake is not. Here the trail is mixed-use, and it sees a fair bit of motorized traffic. This is a popular destination for fishing and scenic views.

THE RUNDOWN

Distance: 10.9 miles point-to-point circuit

Elevation gain: 605 feet south to north, 1,695 north to south

Difficulty: Moderate due to distance to trailhead, length, uneven footing

Hiking time: About 6 hours

Best seasons: Summer, fall

Fees and permits: Free Cloud Peak Wilderness Use Registration

Trail contacts: Bighorn National Forest, 2013 Eastside 2nd St., Sheridan, WY 82801, (307) 674-2600, http://www.fs.usda.gov/bighorn

Maps: USDA Forest Service Bighorn National Forest, National Geographic Trails Unlimited 720 Cloud Peak Wilderness, USGS Willow Park Reservoir

Dog-friendly: Dogs must be under control

Trail surface: Uneven terrain

Nearest town: Big Horn, Wyoming

Other trail users: ATVs outside the wilderness

FINDING THE TRAILHEAD

 This hike connects the Highland Park and Lake Winnie Loop area (Hike 23) with Elk Lake and the Ant Hill Hike (Hike 9). It can also be reached along Kearny Lake Reservoir or Willow Park Reservoir via a network of motorized trails from Penrose Park.

Trailhead GPS: N44 23.702' / W107 03.823'

THE HIKE

For purists hiking the Solitude Loop Trail (Trail 038), this segment represents the longest stretch outside of the Cloud Peak Wilderness. Hikers can expect to encounter a few ATVs along this route, especially at the popular reservoir destinations. You do have a couple of options to deviate from Trail 038. But some sections of motorized route are unavoidable.

Willow Park Reservoir inlet
CHARLES HUBBELL

From the northeast edge of Elk Lake (see Hike 9), Trail 038 heads north, quickly exiting the Cloud Peak Wilderness. Note Trail 219 heads southeast from Elk Lake to Soldier Park from here as well. Just over half a mile later, The Reservoirs segment of the Solitude Loop Trail merges with the ATV route connecting Cloud Peak Reservoir to the southwest with Willow Park Reservoir to the north. The trail follows the west bank of Elk Creek for 0.7 mile. Here, Trail 037 peels off to the west toward Frying Pan Lake. Trail 038 makes a crossing of Elk Creek, and then continues north 3.1 miles to reach the southern end of Willow Park Reservoir. Interestingly, Wyoming Game & Fish have released tiger trout (a brown trout/brook trout hybrid) in Willow Park Reservoir.

Working around the western end of Willow Park Reservoir leads to nonmotorized Trail 118 (see alternative hike option below). From this intersection, Trail 038 continues to follow the reservoir for 0.7 mile, reaching the midway point of the large body of water. The Solitude Loop Trail then departs from the reservoir to climb up and over the ridge to the northwest before dropping down to cross Kearny Creek. The Story Penrose ATV Trail travels northeast at this intersection, while the Solitude Loop Trail heads southwest for 2.5 miles. Tut's Cutoff Trail (Trail 400) connects Trails 118 and 038 here, just north of Beaver Lakes. Sheridan College's Spear-O-Wigwam Campus operates a field camp near here as well, allowing students of all ages to experience backcountry learning and field studies. The Solitude Trail stays north of Kearny Creek as it travels the final 1.4 miles to reach Kearny Lake Reservoir. Here, a 0.3-mile spur connects with the Highland Park and Lake Winnie Trail (Hike 23).

From the southwest edge of Willow Park Reservoir, hikers have the option of heading southwest along Trail 118 to Tut's 038 Cutoff Trail (Trail 400) which leads to Trail 038 north of Beaver Lakes. This alternative route is only open to nonmotorized traffic while the main route (Trail 038) is a multi-use trail between Willow Park and Kearny Lake Reservoirs.

For the more adventurous hikers, modifications to the route can avoid a few sections of the motorized trails between Elk Lake and Kearny Lake as well. Use Trail 130 to connect Elk Lake to the upper 0.5-mile stretch of ATV Trail 082. Follow this to Cloud Peak Reservoir. An obscure footpath leads north of Flatiron Lake, along South Piney Creek, and meets up with Frying Pan Lake. Pick up Trail 037 on the grassy peninsula separating Frying Pan Lake and South Piney Creek. This connects back up with Trail 038 1.3 miles north of Elk Lake.

Cloud Peak Reservoir outlet
CHARLES HUBBELL

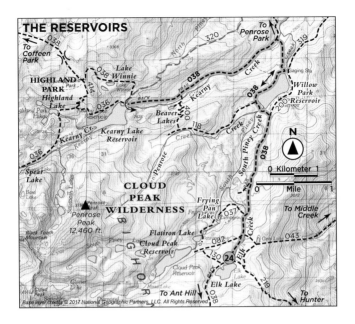

MILES AND DIRECTIONS

0.0 Elk Lake (see Hike 9).

0.5 Junction with Trail 043.

0.6 ATV Trail 082 to Cloud Peak Reservoir.

1.3 Trail 037 to Frying Pan Lake.

4.4 Willow Park Reservoir.

5.0 Trail 118 heads to Tut's Cutoff Trail. Continue on Trail 038.

5.7 Trail departs Willow Park Reservoir toward the northwest.

6.7 Intersection with Story Penrose Trail. Turn left to continue along Solitude Loop Trail (Trail 038).

9.2 Intersection with Tut's 038 Cutoff Trail (Trail 400) north of Beaver Lakes. Continue on Trail 038.

10.6 Kearny Lake Reservoir.

10.9 Junction with Lake Winnie Loop (see Hike 23).

25. FIREBOX PARK, TRAIL 051

WHY GO?

This is a steep hike up an impressive canyon traveling west from the Bud Love Wildlife Management Unit. It provides good access to the large roadless area of the Rock Creek Drainage.

THE RUNDOWN

Distance: 2.8 miles one-way, out-and-back or circuit

Elevation gain: 840 feet

Difficulty: Moderate due to uneven footing and steep inclines

Hiking time: About 4 hours

Best seasons: Summer

Fees and permits: No fees or permits required

Trail contacts: Bighorn National Forest, 2013 Eastside 2nd St., Sheridan, WY 82801, (307) 674-2600, http://www.fs.usda .gov/bighorn; Wyoming Game & Fish Department, 700 Valley View Dr., Sheridan, WY 82801, (307) 672-7418, https://wgfd.wyo .gov/Regional-Offices/Sheridan-Region

Maps: USDA Forest Service Bighorn National Forest, National Geographic Trails Unlimited 720 Cloud Peak Wilderness, USGS Stone Mountain

Dog-friendly: Dogs must be under control

Trail surface: Uneven terrain

Nearest town: Buffalo, Wyoming

Other trail users: Equestrians, especially during hunting season

Special considerations: Bud Love Wildlife Management Area is seasonally closed from Dec 16 to May 14.

FINDING THE TRAILHEAD

Take North Desmet Avenue north out of Buffalo, merging left onto French Creek Road. Follow French Creek Rd. 9 miles to reach the entrance to the Bud Love Wildlife Habitat Management Unit. Follow this dry-weather road 2.4 miles, bearing right at all junctions to reach the trailhead at the Taylor Pond Parking Area.
Trailhead GPS: N44 24.781' / W106 53.250'

THE HIKE

This trail takes off from the Taylor Pond Parking Area of the Bud Love Wildlife Management Area. Here the riparian zone along the stream can harbor both white-tailed and mule deer. The soft purr notes of mountain bluebirds can be

North Sayles Creek Canyon view

sometimes heard as well. In August, grasshoppers are plentiful, and the leaves of a few trees are showing tinges of yellow, hinting at the coming fall.

After a short stroll along the prairie, the hike enters the canyon of North Sayles Creek. The canyon is flanked by dolomite and sandstone pillars and pinnacles carved by erosion. After entering the canyon, the path makes multiple crossings of North Sayles Creek. You should be able to keep your feet dry for all of these. What you can't avoid is the steep terrain. The climb up is intense, and each water crossing makes a convenient location to catch your breath.

As you climb up, North Sayles Creek continues to cascade down. After 1.1 miles, the trail reaches the Bighorn National Forest boundary. From here, the canyon opens up as two stream branches come together. The trail initially crosses the main branch, works its way to a grove of aspen trees, and then doglegs sharply to the northeast to reach the top of a grassy rise. Here, another reef of rock rises above the grasslands. It's worth the extra couple dozen steps to take in the views back down the canyon.

The trail continues to the northwest, crossing Sayles Creek once again. The trail then moves away from the creek as it climbs to the vast grasslands of Firebox Park. Game and cattle trails are almost as well-worn as the hiking trail through parts of the grasslands. Rock outcroppings make interesting photography subjects, and they also double as elevated perches for taking in the surrounding landscape.

Trails fan out from Firebox Park like spokes. The South Rock Creek Trail (Hike 26) connects the HF-Bar Ranch to the wildlands of the entire Rock Creek drainage. The Balm of Gilead Trail provides linkages as well.

Stone Mountain from Firebox Park

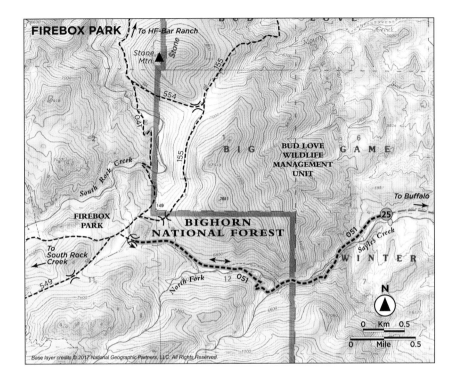

MILES AND DIRECTIONS

0.0 Trailhead on Bud Love Wildlife Management Unit.

0.3 Trail enters the canyon of North Sayles Creek.

1.1 Trail enters Bighorn National Forest.

2.6 Trail crosses pass to enter South Rock Creek drainage.

2.8 Trail joins South Rock Creek Trail in Firebox Park.

26. SOUTH ROCK CREEK, TRAIL 041

WHY GO?

The Rock Creek watershed is an impressive region, much of which lies in a roadless area that borders Cloud Peak Wilderness. The South Rock Creek Trail starts at the historic HF-Bar Ranch and follows the creek to its headwaters.

THE RUNDOWN

Distance: 16.2 miles one-way, out-and-back, or circuit

Elevation gain: 4,580 feet

Difficulty: Strenuous due to distance, elevation gains, and rough trail conditions

Hiking time: About 9 hours

Best seasons: Summer

Fees and permits: Free Cloud Peak Wilderness Use Registration

Trail contacts: Bighorn National Forest, 2013 Eastside 2nd St., Sheridan, WY 82801, (307) 674-2600, http://www.fs.usda.gov/bighorn

Maps: USDA Forest Service Bighorn National Forest, National Geographic Trails Unlimited 720 Cloud Peak Wilderness, USGS Stone Mountain, USGS Hunter Mesa, USGS Lake Angeline, USGS Willow Park Reservoir

Dog-friendly: Dogs must be under control

Trail surface: Uneven terrain

Nearest town: Buffalo, Wyoming

Other trail users: Equestrians

Special considerations: Stay on the trail where this hike crosses private lands

FINDING THE TRAILHEAD

Take North Desmet Avenue north out of Buffalo, merging left onto French Creek Road. Follow French Creek for 11 miles, passing the Bud Love Wildlife Habitat Management Unit along the way. Turn west (left) where French Creek Road intersects Rock Creek Road. You'll drive under the HF-Bar Arch here. Continue 2.2 miles along the county road to reach the HF-Bar Ranch complex. Hang a left to reach the barn and corrals. Drive between these and park behind the barn. Parking is behind the left green gate. The trail takes off through the right green gate.

Trailhead GPS: N44 27.406' / W106 53.987'

THE HIKE

The South Rock Creek Trail (Trail 041) starts at the HF-Bar Ranch north of Buffalo. Access to this private property is granted through an easement. Please respect the landowners and the property. Park in the designated parking area, keep gates as you found them, and always stick to the established trail.

The trail is well marked with signs from the HF–Bar Ranch. It crosses through a gate and follows the road initially, before splitting off to the right and entering the short but spectacular canyon of South Rock Creek. The vertical slabs of sedimentary rock rise like towering walls. The burned timber from the 2012 Gilead Fire adds an element of contrast to the landscape.

The trail makes multiple knee-deep fords of South Rock Creek. This can be especially tricky considering the swift nature of the current. After passing through the canyon, the trail crosses the boundary into the Bighorn National Forest. The trail splits here, with the right branch leading to Balm of Gilead and Spring Creeks. The main branch travels south and westward (to the left) to cross South Rock Creek once again before switchbacking steadily upward. After a steep initial climb, the grade eases, eventually topping out on a flank of Stone Mountain. Broad grasslands, giant ponderosa pine, and immense reefs of sedimentary rock make for dramatic photos.

The trail crosses another high finger, holds the contour for a time, and then descends down through dorm room–sized boulder shrapnel that has fallen from the face of Stone Mountain. At the bottom of the grade, the Stone Mountain cutoff trail heads southward. The main trail crosses South Rock Creek to reach a nice meadow, a worthy campsite by any measure.

The path continues in a steady climb from here, then, a brief jog north leads to yet another crossing. Beyond here, the trail switchbacks up through the trees, emerging into open grasslands where the trail becomes faint at best. Eventually, it intersects the Stone Mountain Trail and Firebox Park in a high and grassy saddle. From the heart of the park, the South Rock Creek Trail continues down toward the valley floor. The path drops into a bottomland clearing, crosses several spring fed trickles, then turns west to follow South Rock Creek.

From here, the trail maintains a course through lodgepole pines, eventually reaching the confluence of Middle Rock Creek. The trail crosses South Rock Creek and rises to a clearing. A sign marks the junction with the Middle Rock Creek and Balm of Gilead Trails. The South Rock Creek Trail continues west and south. It next reaches Trail 549, an alternate trail from Firebox Park. A mix of spruce and aspen now fill in the bottomlands.

While other trails continue to offshoot, the South Rock Creek Trail continues to follow the namesake body of water, making multiple crossings. It tops out at a ridgetop near the end of FR 399. Ant Hill is the prominent summit to the west. The trail dips, crosses South Rock Creek for the final time, and then zigzags up the wooded drainage to the north. Look for the cutoff trail that runs south toward Triangle Park. Bear right (northwest) here and finish with a vigorous climb. The South Rock Creek Trail merges with the Elk Lake Trail (Trail 219). Travel

South Rock Creek Trail
from HF-Bar Ranch

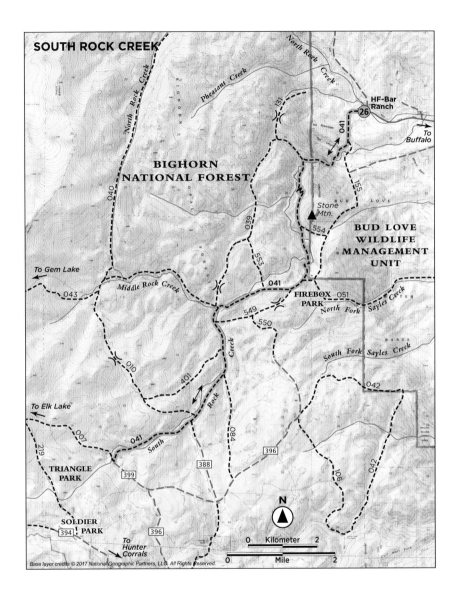

northwest (to the right) on this for 2.6 miles to reach the Solitude Loop Trail (Trail 038) at Elk Lake. The Ant Hill Route (Hike 9) and The Reservoirs (Hike 24) take off from Elk Lake. Remember, if you are taking this trail all the way to the Cloud Peak Wilderness, a self-registration permit is required.

MILES AND DIRECTIONS

0.0 Trailhead at HF-Bar Ranch. Follow signs and stick to roadway and trail.

1.0 Trail enters the canyon.

1.7 Trail enters Bighorn National Forest.

1.8 Junction with Balm of Gilead Trail (039).

3.6 Junction with cutoff to Stone Mountain (554). Bear right and descend.

4.8 Junction with Stone Mountain Trail. Turn right as the trail enters Firebox Park.

6.7 Junction with Middle Rock Creek Trail (043).

7.2 Junction with cutoff trail from Firebox Park (549).

7.9 Junction with spike of South Rock Creek Trail (401).

8.9 Junction with Bear Gulch Trail (084).

9.1 Junction with cutoff trail (010) to Middle Rock Creek.

10.8 Junction with FR 399. Turn right and descend to ford creek at South Rock Creek Cutoff Trail (007).

13.6 Trail joins Elk Lake Trail (Trail 219).

16.2 Elk Lake.

NORTHERN WILDERNESS ACCESS ADDITIONAL HIKES

The Shell Lakes Trail (Trail 032) and the **Shell Lakes High Trail** (Trail 828) both connect FR 280 to Shell Lake. Trail 032 continues southeast to the Lakes of the Rough and Edelman Pass. These trails can also be reached by hiking the **Shell Creek Trail** (Trail 057) and FR 271 past Adelaide Lake from the Adelaide Trailhead near the Shell Ranger Station and the Ranger Creek Campground.

Little Goose Trail (Trail 027) begins at the end of the steep and rugged FR 314 (south of Little Goose Campground). The trail ends at the Solitude Loop Trail (Trail 038) between Coffeen Park Trailhead and Highland Park (see Hike 23).

The Story Penrose Trail (Trail 033) from Story is a popular ATV trail that provides access to the Penrose and Little Goose areas. There is no motorized travel on the trail early in the season, and it makes a nice hike then.

The South Piney Trail (Trail 626) is a short trail that provides easy access to the forest. It takes off from the Story Fish Hatchery and follows South Piney Creek.

The Story Penrose Trail makes a great early-season hike

RED GRADE TO SHELL

Improvements to Red Grade Road are continually being made, but this will always be a steep, winding, and rough road. It makes a scenic alternative to US Hwy. 14, and Red Grade Road intersects this highway south of Burgess Junction. Red Grade is popular with ATV riders and it provides access to numerous suitable trails. Hikers will find additional routes to Geddes Lake, Sawmill Lakes, and Coney Lakes—all fishable bodies of water.

Old Mail Trail is off of FR 17 and travels part of the historic route connecting Big Horn to Hyattville. The mail delivery route was phased out when the railroads moved in.

The Shell Falls Interpretive Site is right off of US 14. Here visitors can see the magnificent falls while learning about the area's flora and fauna. (Note the visitor center is closed seasonally.) The Bench Trail traverses the lands south of US 14, while the Cedar Creek Trail penetrates the territory to the north of the highway, traveling under iconic Copmans Tomb.

Shell Creek flowing through Shell Canyon

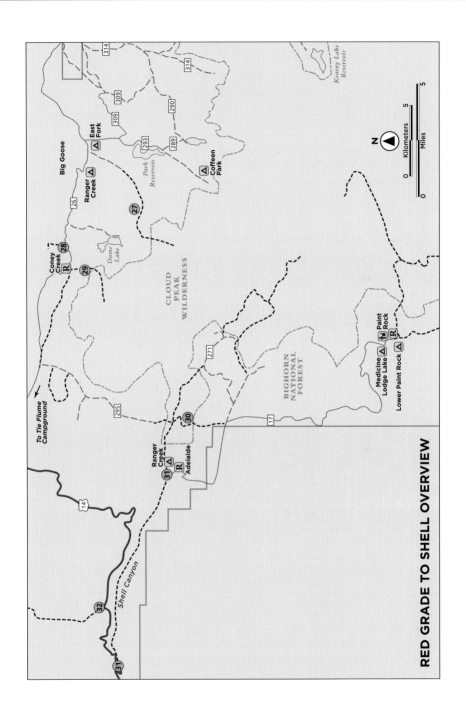

RED GRADE TO SHELL OVERVIEW

27. GEDDES LAKE, TRAIL 023

WHY GO?

This trail visits a picturesque lake in one of the lesser-used corners of Cloud Peak Wilderness. The trail is open to motorized travel to Weston Reservoir, but beyond that, it is limited to nonmotorized uses.

THE RUNDOWN

Distance: 7.6 miles round trip, out-and-back

Elevation gain: 1,390 feet

Difficulty: Moderate due to distance, elevation gains, and uneven footing

Hiking time: About 4 hours

Best seasons: Late spring, summer, early fall

Fees and permits: Free Cloud Peak Wilderness Use Registration

Trail contacts: Bighorn National Forest, 2013 Eastside 2nd St., Sheridan, WY 82801, (307) 674-2600, http://www.fs.usda.gov/bighorn

Maps: USDA Forest Service Bighorn National Forest, National Geographic Trails Unlimited 720 Cloud Peak Wilderness, USGS Park Reservoir, USGS Dome Lake

Dog-friendly: Dogs must be under control

Trail surface: Uneven terrain

Nearest town: Big Horn, Wyoming

Other trail users: ATVs to Weston Reservoir

FINDING THE TRAILHEAD

Take Red Grade Road/FR 26 (either from US Hwy. 14 or from Big Horn) to just east of the Big Goose Ranger Station. Turn south onto FR 299. After 0.8 mile, bear left at the junction and follow the road. Four-wheel drive is recommended. The road eventually turns into motorized Trail 023. Beyond Weston Reservoir, Trail 023 is limited to nonmotorized uses.
Trailhead GPS: N44 33.787' / W107 15.754'

THE HIKE

This hike enters Cloud Peak Wilderness, so you'll need to obtain a free permit at a major trailhead, ranger station, or Forest Service office before you begin.

Many find it best to park along FR 299 and hike the rocky road for a ways. Babione Creek provides suitable moose habitat, so whether traveling by foot or tire, be sure to watch for the largest member of the deer family.

Moose twins

From the end of FR 299, mixed-use Trail 023 leads to Weston Reservoir. The trail is open to nonmotorized travel beyond Weston Reservoir. Passing along the southern shores of the reservoir, nonmotorized Trail 023 continues west initially. It passes great moose meadows above Weston Reservoir before taking a dogleg to the southwest. Views of Elk Peak and Saddle Mountain are visible to the west as the trail turns south.

The trail climbs upward as it continues through the pine forests, crossing into the Cloud Peak Wilderness about halfway between Weston Reservoir and Geddes Lake. A short drop puts you into the drainage of the West Fork of Big Goose Creek. The pines thin out as you approach Lake Mirage, a shallow pond with equal parts boulders and water.

The trail crosses the creek at the foot of the next pond. Here it continues through the trees eventually coming to the western end of Geddes Lake. The forested spine of Black Rib rises to the south.

Wyoming State Flower:
Indian Paintbrush

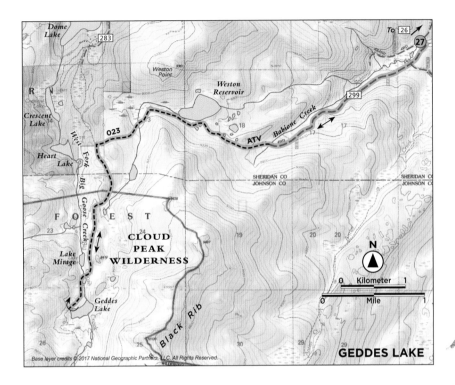

GEDDES LAKE

MILES AND DIRECTIONS

0.0 Start at the Babione Creek crossing of FR 299.

0.1 FR 299 turns into multi-use Trail 023.

0.6 Weston Reservoir. Trail 023 is nonmotorized beyond here.

3.2 Lake Mirage.

3.8 Geddes Lake.

28. SAWMILL LAKES, TRAIL 022

WHY GO?

A pleasant stroll under a forested canopy, the flows of the West Fork of Big Goose Creek lie to the east of the trail. The trail bisects the Sawmill Lakes and ends at the dam of Sawmill Reservoir.

THE RUNDOWN

Distance: 2.2 miles out-and-back

Elevation gain: Minimal

Difficulty: Easy due to shorter distance with relatively flat walking

Hiking time: About 1 hour

Best seasons: Late spring, summer, early fall

Fees and permits: No fees or permits are required

Trail contacts: Bighorn National Forest, 2013 Eastside 2nd St., Sheridan, WY 82801, (307) 674-2600, http://www.fs.usda.gov/bighorn

Maps: USDA Forest Service Bighorn National Forest, National Geographic Trails Unlimited 720 Cloud Peak Wilderness, USGS Walker Mountain, USGS Dome Lake

Dog-friendly: Dogs must be under control

Trail surface: Uneven terrain

Nearest town: Big Horn, Wyoming

Other trail users: None

FINDING THE TRAILHEAD

Take Red Grade Road/FR 26 (either from US Hwy. 14 or from Big Horn) to the turn for Twin Lakes Picnic Area. There is parking for about a half a dozen vehicles on the south side of FR 26 just west of Big Goose Creek bridge and on the east side of the road that leads to Twin Lakes Reservoir. Additional parking can be found off the side road just east of the bridge. The trailhead is on the north side of the road, and the trail runs down the west bank of the creek.

Trailhead GPS: N44 36.778' / W107 17.965'

THE HIKE

This hike can get you to three fishing spots in just over one mile so don't let the crowded parking lot intimidate you.

The trail takes off into the woods north of Red Grade Road/FR 26. You'll maintain altitude along a glacial lateral moraine as the West Fork of Big Goose

Creek flows below. It's about three quarters of a mile to the Sawmill Lakes. The trail hooks west here and continues on for another quarter of a mile to the dam of Sawmill Reservoir.

Yellowstone cutthroat trout are occasionally stocked in the Sawmill Lakes, and Snake River cutts are also present. The fish average 10–15 inches. Splake, a lake trout/brook trout hybrid, are occasionally caught in the Sawmill Lakes. Splake have also been stocked in Sawmill Reservoir, which also has a large population of small brook trout. These lakes are rimmed with trees, so you'll get plenty of experience roll casting if you are fly-fishing. Tossing lures is also productive.

Trail 417 looks tempting on the map, but it is a lesser trail. It is poorly marked and easily missed from the Red Grade Road. The hike is more rugged, and overall it's not really worth it. Do yourself a favor and stick to Trail 022.

Sawmill Lake Reservoir
ROHY KEFFER

Sawmill Lakes
ROHY KEFFER

Sawmill Lakes
ROHY KEFFER

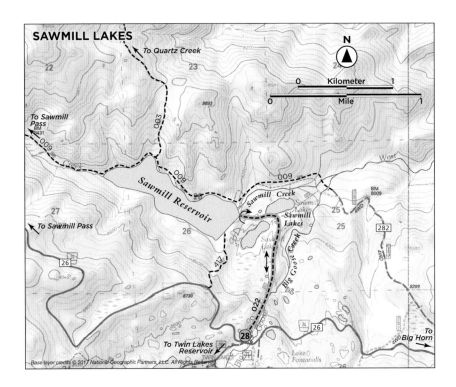

MILES AND DIRECTIONS

0.0 Trailhead.

0.7 Big Sawmill Lake.

0.8 Little Sawmill Lake.

1.1 Trail reaches the dam of Sawmill Reservoir.

29. CONEY LAKE, TRAIL 021

WHY GO?

An easy day trip off of Red Grade Road, this trail enters the most northerly pocket of the Cloud Peak Wilderness at the Stull Lakes and continues on to Coney Lake. While the highest peaks are farther south, the scenery here of tree-lined lakes with surrounding peaks that flirt with the timberline is equally impressive.

THE RUNDOWN

Distance: 1.6 miles one-way to Stull Lakes, 3.7 miles one-way to Coney Lake, out-and-back

Elevation gain: 640 feet

Difficulty: Easy to Stull Lakes, Moderate to Coney Lake due to longer distance and uneven footing

Hiking time: About 4 hours

Best seasons: Late spring, summer, fall

Fees and permits: Free Cloud Peak Wilderness Use Registration

Trail contacts: Bighorn National Forest, 2013 Eastside 2nd St.,

Sheridan, WY 82801, (307) 674-2600, http://www.fs.usda.gov/bighorn

Maps: USDA Forest Service Bighorn National Forest, National Geographic Trails Unlimited 720 Cloud Peak Wilderness, USGS Dome Lake

Dog-friendly: Dogs must be under control

Trail surface: Uneven terrain

Nearest town: Big Horn, Wyoming

Other trail users: None

FINDING THE TRAILHEAD

The Coney Lake Trailhead is a well-marked destination off of Red Grade Road/FR 26. It is 16 miles east of US Hwy. 14 and just east of Rock Chuck Pass. It can also be reached following the Red Grade Road from Big Horn, where it is just west of the Twin Lakes Picnic Area.
Trailhead GPS: N44 36.865' / W107 19.442'

THE HIKE

From the well-marked parking lot, cross the Red Grade Road to the trailhead. Enter the timber and after two tenths of a mile, maintain a straight course as you cross Trail 418 running from Twin Lakes to Rock Chuck Pass. Half a mile from the trailhead, you'll cross the trickle that is Snail Creek, and beyond that, you'll walk beyond the wet meadow that contains the small Lost Lake. Lost Lake is not

Mule deer fawn in timber

much more than a wide spot along the water east of the trail. Like most water in the Bighorns, these places hold stunted brook trout if you are so inclined to cast a line. Or you can keep your rod packed up until you reach Coney Creek and the Stull Lakes a mile or so ahead.

The trail cuts between the Stull Lakes and heads west toward Coney Lake. The trail picks up some elevation as it climbs a finger ridge. A second steep pitch eventually leads to a grassy meadow and Coney Lake beyond. Coney Lake is a classic picturesque scene of scattered boulders and brook trout breaking the surface of a mountain pond that is tucked up along the base of an impressive domed peak. While most of the fish in Coney Lake won't ever grow to 12 inches, they sure are fun to catch.

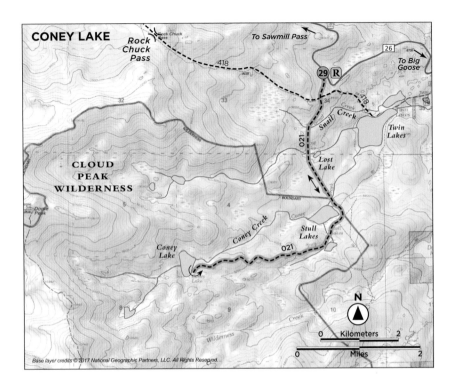

MILES AND DIRECTIONS

0.0 Coney Creek Trailhead.

0.2 Junction with Rock Chuck Pass Trail. Continue straight ahead.

0.5 Trail crosses Snail Creek.

1.5 Trail crosses Coney Creek.

1.6 Big Stull Lake.

2.0 Little Stull Lake.

3.7 Coney Lake.

30. OLD MAIL TRAIL, TRAIL 817

WHY GO?

This route follows the old Big Horn Toll Road, the historic mail and stagecoach route connecting Big Horn and Hyattville in the late 1800s. Both the northern and southern segments of this hike are open to motorized ATV travel; however, the middle section can provide a wilderness experience in some of the lower elevations of the Cloud Peak Wilderness.

THE RUNDOWN

Distance: 5.1 miles one-way, point-to-point or out-and-back

Elevation gain: 625 feet

Difficulty: Moderate due to distance and uneven footing

Hiking time: About 5 hours

Best seasons: Summer, fall

Fees and permits: Free Cloud Peak Wilderness Use Registration

Trail contacts: Bighorn National Forest, 2013 Eastside 2nd St., Sheridan, WY 82801, (307) 674-2600, http://www.fs.usda.gov/bighorn

Maps: USDA Forest Service Bighorn National Forest, National Geographic Trails Unlimited 720 Cloud Peak Wilderness, USGS Shell Reservoir

Dog-friendly: Dogs must be under control

Trail surface: Uneven terrain

Nearest town: Big Horn, Wyoming

Other trail users: Equestrians, ATVs on sections outside the wilderness area

FINDING THE TRAILHEAD

Take FR 17 off of US Hwy. 14 for 10 miles, passing the Shell Ranger Station 2.8 miles in. Park at the junction with FR 271. The trail heads north from here. To reach the northern trailhead, just east of the Ranger Station, take FR 277 initially and then FR 226. High clearance is recommended for these primitive roads.

Trailhead GPS: N44 30.344' / W107 27.279'

THE HIKE

The Old Mail Trail follows the historic route of the Big Horn Toll Road. The stagecoach route connected the communities of Big Horn and Hyattville in the late 1800s. The road was phased out by 1901 when the railroad built a spur south of Lovell.

The southern reaches of the route follow along Crooked Creek, while the northern segment requires multiple creek crossings of Moraine, McKinnon, Mail, and Shell Creeks.

Access roads to both ends of the Old Mail Trail can be impassable for low clearance vehicles. Another option is to park at the trailhead just east of the Shell Creek Ranger Station. Here the Adelaide Trail, also called the Shell Creek Trail

Hoary Balsamroot
MOLLY MCKAY

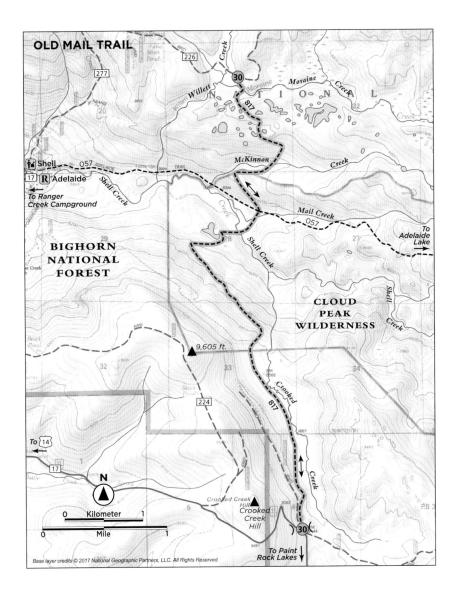

(Trail 057), runs to the east. Like the northern and southern stretches of Trail 817, this trail is also a motorcycle trail until it reaches the boundary of the Cloud Peak Wilderness (1.4 miles). From the boundary, it is a 0.4-mile walk to reach the intersection of the Old Mail Trail. From here, the Adelaide Trail continues east along Mail Creek initially, then heads southeast, crossing Adelaide Creek, before eventually exiting the wilderness area just west of Adelaide Lake.

When hiking from the south, the Old Mail trail begins off of FR 17. Note FR 17 travels through a section of private property before reaching the trailhead. Respect the landowner by sticking to the road. And like many primitive roads in the region, this one is best avoided during inclement weather.

The trail heads down (north) along the valley of Crooked Creek. Cattle may share these mountain pastures. A fence and gate marks the boundary of the Cloud Peak Wilderness. From here, the historic wagon road travels northwest descending across steep slopes timbered with spruce and fir. About a mile into the wilderness, the trail makes a sharp turn to the east. It can be faint in the meadows as it travels past a nameless puddle of water. It turns north/northeast traversing some swampy sections, before materializing again as it drops across timbered slopes to reach first Shell and then Mail Creeks.

Next up is the intersection with the Adelaide Trail. From here, the Old Mail Trail continues northwest along the 100-plus year old route, now gaining in elevation with every step. The trail initially travels through sagebrush meadows and eventually enters a stand of aspen. From here, the hike exits the Cloud Peak Wilderness. The final 1.1 miles once again follow an ATV trail as it crosses McKinnon Creek and then weaves among multiple woodland ponds. A final crossing at Moraine Creek leads to FR 226.

MILES AND DIRECTIONS

0.0 Crooked Creek Trailhead. Follow lower roadway toward Crooked Creek.

1.6 Trail leaves Crooked Creek Valley and enters Cloud Peak Wilderness. Beginning of descent toward Shell Creek.

2.9 Trail reaches the shore of nameless lake.

3.1 Trail fords Shell Creek.

3.3 Trail crosses Mail Creek.

3.4 Two junctions with the Adelaide Lake Trail. Follow the old road grade that climbs northwest.

3.9 Trail leaves Cloud Peak Wilderness.

4.2 Trail crosses McKinnon Creek.

5.0 Trail fords Moraine Creek.

5.1 Trail joins FR 226.

31. BENCH TRAIL, TRAIL 184

WHY GO?

The Bench Trail is a popular biking route, and it is just as great for hiking. Sticking south of US Hwy. 14, it travels along Shell Canyon from Ranger Creek Campground to the Post Creek Picnic Area. It crosses through the historic tornado path of 1959 as well as the Shell Creek Research Natural Area.

THE RUNDOWN

Distance: 10 miles one-way, point-to-point or out-and-back

Elevation gain: 2,550 feet

Difficulty: Moderate east to west, strenuous west to east due to elevation gains

Hiking time: About 5 hours

Best seasons: Spring, summer, fall

Fees and permits: No fees or permits required

Trail contacts: Bighorn National Forest, 2013 Eastside 2nd St., Sheridan, WY 82801, (307) 674-2600, http://www.fs.usda.gov/bighorn

Maps: USDA Forest Service Bighorn National Forest, USGS Shell Falls, USGS Black Mountain

Dog-friendly: Dogs must be under control

Trail surface: Uneven terrain

Nearest town: Shell, Wyoming

Other trail users: Mountain bikers

Special considerations: This is Trail 184, but it is mislabeled as Trail 084 in many locations. Don't let Trail 084 references confuse you; you're on the right path.

FINDING THE TRAILHEAD

Take FR 17 from US Hwy. 14. After 2.8 miles, you reach the Ranger Creek Campground. Drive into the campground and take the first left to reach the trailhead. The trail ends at Post Creek Picnic Area at mile 22.8 on US 14.

Trailhead GPS: N44 32.731' / W107 30.053'

THE HIKE

Shell Canyon, named for the shell fossils found in the sedimentary rock walls of the canyon, is a scenic drive, but to fully appreciate its beauty, slow the pace down a bit and hike the Bench Trail. Much of the hike is under the canopy of forest, but gaps in the trees provide canyon vistas including looks at Copmans Tomb (see Hike 32) on the opposite side of the valley.

In June 1959, a tornado ripped over the ridge and down the slopes to Granite Creek. This disturbance tragically stuck the site of a campground and took the life of one person. Downed timber can still be seen, although much of the area has returned to forest under the natural process of succession.

If you are limited to one vehicle, an out-and-back from Ranger Creek to the site of a 1959 tornado would make a lovely 12-mile round trip hike. The trail maintains much of its elevation for this stretch. Beyond the tornado site, the remainder of the trail drops a couple thousand feet, so it is advisable to run a shuttle from Post Creek if a second vehicle is available. Otherwise, you're looking at quite an uphill slog on the return hike.

Fire can play a natural role in the landscape; however, human-caused fires have also shaped the slopes in this area. Sheep ranchers set blazes to the drainage as far back as the 1890s in an attempt to create additional grazing pastures for their flocks. In 1984, illegal fireworks ignited a blaze that quickly burned from the highway to the ridgetop.

Another disturbance in the area has affected the stands of Douglas-fir in this drainage. Many trees were lost to a bark beetle outbreak in the early 2000s.

The western most stretches of the Bench Trail drop in elevation. The landscape shifts to juniper and steppe grasslands dotted with sagebrush. Views open up and Copmans Tomb draws the most attention.

Early in the season, arrowleaf balsamroot is common to elevations of 8,000 feet

Bench Trail Ranger
Creek Trailhead

TRAIL
US
National
Forest
184

The stretch of trail nearest to the Post Creek parking lot passes through Shell Creek Research Natural Area. This area was designated in 1987 and highlights a diversity of plants, including Rocky Mountain juniper, black sagebrush, and blue-bunch wheatgrass.

The western terminus of the Bench Trail is at the Post Creek parking area. Fed by springs, Post Creek is a green oasis in a fairly dry landscape.

MILES AND DIRECTIONS

0.0   Trailhead in Ranger Creek Campground.

1.0   Trail passes Shell Creek Campground.

1.5   Trail passes privately leased cabin.

2.3   Junction with spur to the top of Lake Ridge. Stay right.

6.0   Tornado site.

8.0   Trail crosses 1984 fire site.

10.0 Trail emerges at Post Creek day-use area.

32. **CEDAR CREEK, TRAIL 055**

WHY GO?
While the Bench Trail (Hike 31) offers up views of Shell Canyon and Copmans Tomb, the Cedar Creek Trail takes you right up to the base of this distinctive ridge. Despite being a neat trip, this trail receives minimal hiking pressure.

THE RUNDOWN

Distance: 8 miles out-and-back

Elevation gain: 1,095 feet

Difficulty: Moderate due to distance and uneven footing

Hiking time: About 4 hours

Best seasons: Spring, summer, fall

Fees and permits: No fees or permits

Trail contacts: Bighorn National Forest, 2013 Eastside 2nd St., Sheridan, WY 82801, (307)

674-2600, http://www.fs.usda.gov/bighorn

Maps: USDA Forest Service Bighorn National Forest, USGS Shell Falls, USGS Black Mountain, USGS Hidden Teepee Creek

Dog-friendly: Dogs must be under control

Trail surface: Uneven terrain

Nearest town: Shell, Wyoming

Other trail users: None

FINDING THE TRAILHEAD
 Just east of the Shell Falls on US Hwy. 14, take FR 264 to the north. High clearance and four-wheel drive recommended for this 2-mile stretch of road. Or you can hike in from near the highway.
Trailhead GPS: N44 35.589' / W107 37.697'

THE HIKE
This path goes over some rough country below the face of Copmans Tomb, the dominant dolomite and limestone bluff rising above Shell Falls. It is named after a local settler and inventor, Wolfgang Robert Copman, better known as Jack, who had aspirations of launching a flying glider from the butte. He never realized his dream of flying off the peak. Nor was his wish for his ashes to be scattered from a flying machine granted. Instead, Mr. Copman was buried in nearby Greybull following his death in 1907.

Copmans Tomb

The Cedar Creek Trail (Trail 055) is an out-and-back hike that can be done in a day or stretched into an easy overnighter. The lower elevations make it an appealing early-season hike, while the higher country continues to thaw out.

East of Shell Falls, FR 264 takes off to the north of US Hwy. 14. This is a rutted, high clearance road, so it might be wise to hike the 2-mile stretch to Brindle Creek. A quarter of a mile past Brindle Creek, a track splits away from the road as it heads north (to the right) toward Copmans Tomb.

The Beef Trail (Trail 056) continues straight ahead. The Beef Trail is south of the Cedar Creek Trail and roughly parallels the highway initially as it crosses Fender Creek and then doglegs around a canyon along the lower stretches of Cedar Creek before shanking off to the southwest, eventually reaching the highway.

The Cedar Creek Trail takes the right turn up to a small out-of-place pond. Keeping along the western edge of the puddle, it continues northwest up the open ridgeline where it meets up with a second roadbed near the dry wash of Survey Creek. The route continues climbing steadily, eventually crossing a divide and dipping down to Fender Creek.

Look for the trunk of Elephant Head Rock standing out prominently off of Sunlight Mesa. The Cedar Creek Trail heads north shortly after crossing Fender Creek, a seasonal body of water some years. The trail charts a route along the high shoulders of Copmans Tomb for 2.3 miles, eventually reaching a meadow.

From here, the route drops down to the Cedar Creek bottoms. One could spend a fair bit of time exploring the area, and Cedar Creek makes a lovely camping spot.

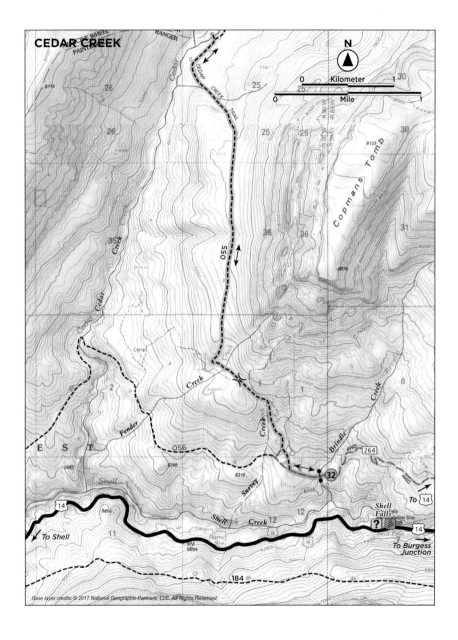

CEDAR CREEK

N

0   Kilometer   1
0   Mile   1

MILES AND DIRECTIONS

0.0 Trail starts out heading west along FR 264 at Brindle Creek.

0.2 Trail heads north, splitting away from the old road.

0.9 Cross dry wash of Survey Creek.

1.2 Cross Fender Creek drainage and continue northward.

4.0 Reach Cedar Creek.

RED GRADE TO SHELL ADDITIONAL HIKES

Rock Chuck Pass (Trail 418) connects Sawmill Pass and the Coney Creek Trailhead. The route is faint in places, especially the eastern stretches. The views from the pristine mountain meadows are top-notch.

Copper Creek (Trail 424) is a 1.8-mile one-way trail near the Tie Flume Campground. It connects FR 16 and the multi-use Tie/Prune Trail (Trail 430). The route follows the South Tongue River and crosses Copper Creek.

Beef Trail (Trail 056) is primarily used as a stock trail. It parallels north of US Hwy. 14 through Shell Canyon and offers up impressive views of Elephant Head Rock and Copmans Tomb. The Cedar Creek Trail (Trail 55, Hike 32) heads north from the eastern end of this trail.

NORTHEAST BIGHORNS

Extensive grassland parks characterize the northern reaches of the Bighorn Mountains. The prairie foothills stretch behind short but ruggedly stunning canyons of tall reefs of sedimentary rocks. Access on the eastern front can be limited by private land, but approaches from the north, west, and south are possible. Walker Prairie, Wolf Creek, and Horseshoe Mountain can be strung together making a backpacking trip, or the areas can be explored as day trips.

Steamboat Point and Black Mountain Lookout Tower are both prominent features off of US Hwy. 14. These day trips provide incredible views from high perches, and despite their steep grades, can provide fairly short trips for enthusiastic young hikers.

Tongue River Canyon is a crowded thoroughfare in the lower reaches, but the crowds dissipate the farther from the trailhead you travel. One could theoretically hike from the Tongue River Trailhead all the way to Burgess Junction, but most visitors are only headed as far as the cave.

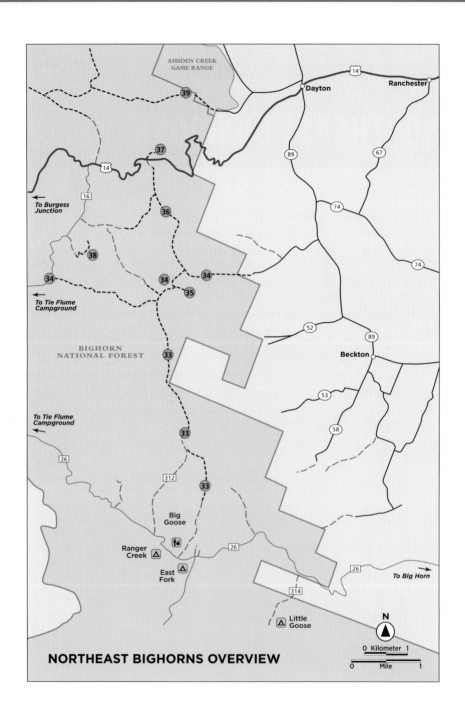

NORTHEAST BIGHORNS OVERVIEW

33. WALKER PRAIRIE, TRAIL 014

WHY GO?

Walker Prairie is the largest expanse of grasslands within the eastern foothills of the Bighorns. It provides impressive views, and massive sandstone reefs dot the landscape.

THE RUNDOWN

Distance: 11.1 miles one-way, out-and-back or circuit

Elevation gain: 2,155 feet

Difficulty: Moderate due to distance, elevation, and uneven footing

Hiking time: About 10 hours

Best seasons: Spring, fall

Fees and permits: No fees or permits required

Trail contacts: Bighorn National Forest, 2013 Eastside 2nd St., Sheridan, WY 82801, (307) 674-

2600, http://www.fs.usda.gov/bighorn

Maps: USDA Forest Service Bighorn National Forest, National Geographic Trails Unlimited 720 Cloud Peak Wilderness, USGS Beckton, USGS Park Reservoir, USGS Walker Mountain

Dog-friendly: Dogs must be under control

Trail surface: Uneven terrain

Nearest town: Big Horn, Wyoming

Other trail users: Equestrians

FINDING THE TRAILHEAD

Take Red Grade Road/FR 26 (either from US Hwy. 14 or from Big Horn) to the Big Goose Ranger Station. Follow FR 296 north (high clearance recommended) to reach the southern trailhead. The northern end of the trail connects with the Wolf Creek Trail (Hike 34).
Trailhead GPS: N44 37.403' / W107 12.706'

THE HIKE

Walker Prairie is the largest expanse of grasslands within the eastern foothills of the Bighorns. Alternative access to the northern end of the prairie can be reached via the Wolf Creek Trail (Trail 001, Hike 34), Hendrick Ridge Trail (Trail 005, Hike 36), or Trail 003 from Sawmill Reservoir. Be aware that grazing leases occur in parts of Walker Prairie. Cattle should be expected during summer visits.

The Walker Prairie route (Trail 014) begins with a short climb and then a steady decline along the ridgeline. It bottoms out at the East Fork of Big Goose Creek, hugging the western bank for a stretch before making two water crossings. A side trip along an unofficial trail follows the East Fork to a waterfall.

Grassland meadows make for impressive viewsheds. Take in the craggy mountain peaks of the Cloud Peak Wilderness. The rugged canyon of Big Goose Creek offers up a contrasting view toward the north and east. The main trail bends west to intersect with FR 312. Follow this primitive road to the right, reaching the end of it in about half a mile. The trail then plummets down the hillside to reach the West Fork of Big Goose Creek. After crossing this, the climb is steep for a stretch. Hike through the grasslands and over the saddle to reach the Prairie Creek drainage. You'll cross Prairie Creek, and then ford Wolf Creek near where the two streams come together.

As you continue to climb, Walker Prairie opens up around you. Porous limestone allows rainfall to percolate quickly, ensuring grasses are the dominant vegetation here. Southern views offer superb looks at Dome Peak, and jagged Black Tooth Mountain. The exposed faces of She Bear and Walker Mountains loom to the north. While the Soldier Creek Trail heads northeast and crosses into private property, the main trail continues westward, passing near a primitive cow camp along Wolf Creek before climbing vigorously up the grassy draw approaching the base of Walker Mountain.

The trail next crosses the divide to enter the Quartz Creek watershed. Near panoramic views are the rewards as the sandstone reefs of Little and Big Mountain rise above. You'll continue hiking onward. The Walker Prairie Trail intersects the Wolf Creek Trail (Trail 001, Hike 34) near the confluence of Quartz and Wolf Creeks.

Little Mountain

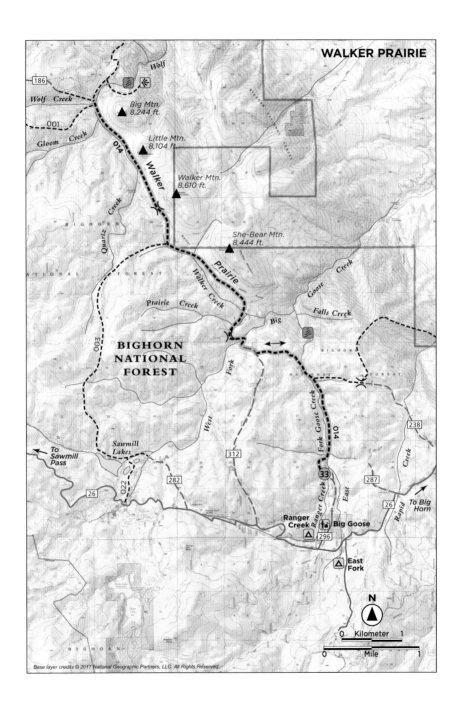

MILES AND DIRECTIONS

0.0   Trailhead at end of FR 296.

1.2   First compulsory ford of East Fork of Big Goose Creek. Trail now follows east bank.

2.3   Junction with cutoff trail to Rapid Creek. Continue straight ahead.

2.5   Trail fords the East Fork, then climbs westward.

3.7   Trail joins FR 312. Turn right and follow road downward.

4.2   End of FR 312. Turn right and follow road downward.

4.3   Bridge over West Fork of Big Goose Creek.

4.6   Trail crosses the divide into Prairie Creek drainage.

4.8   Trail crosses Prairie Creek.

5.0   Trail fords Walker creek and starts climbing into Walker Prairie.

5.3   Junction with Big Goose Trail. Turn left.

6.9   Trail crosses Buck Creek to join Soldier Creek Trail. Bear left.

8.4   Trail crosses divide to enter Quartz Creek watershed.

11.0   Trail fords Quartz Creek.

11.1   End of Walker Prairie Trail. Wolf Creek Trail runs north.

34. **WOLF CREEK, TRAIL 001**

WHY GO?

There is no denying that this is trail #1. Literally. It is Trail 001. The Wolf Creek Trail traverses a swath of the eastern Bighorn Mountains from the logged hillsides south of Black Mountain, down to the confluence of Quartz and Wolf Creeks, and on down to the Bighorn National Forest Boundary and to Eatons' Guest Ranch in the east. It provides a route to the northern stretches of Walker Prairie (Hike 33).

THE RUNDOWN

Distance: 11.6 miles one-way, out-and-back or point-to-point

Elevation gain: 740 feet

Difficulty: Moderate due to distance, elevation gains, and uneven terrain

Hiking time:

Best seasons: Late spring, summer, early fall

Fees and permits: No fees or permits required

Trail contacts: Bighorn National Forest, 2013 Eastside 2nd St., Sheridan, WY 82801, (307) 674-2600, http://www.fs.usda.gov/bighorn

Maps: USDA Forest Service Bighorn National Forest, USGS Wolf, USGS Dayton South, USGS Walker Mountain

Dog-friendly: Dogs must be under control

Trail surface: Uneven trail, logging road

Nearest town: Dayton or Big Horn, Wyoming

Other trail users: Equestrians

Special considerations: This hike describes the western trailhead. The eastern end of the Wolf Creek Trail crosses private property before reaching the Bighorn National Forest Boundary. Eatons' Guest Ranch generously provides limited access to the trail, but access can be restricted. Contact the Bighorn National Forest to determine current access. Trail 001 can also be reached from Steamboat Point via Trail 005 (Hike 36) or off of FR 16.

FINDING THE TRAILHEAD

Take US Hwy. 14 to FR 16 between Dayton and Burgess Junction. FR 16 is a solid road, although the side roads off of it can be a bit dicey. Head south on FR 16 for 6.2 miles. Then turn left (east) to travel on FR 223 for about a mile. Merge onto FR 211218 to reach the trailhead. There is limited parking at the end, but there are a few pullouts along the 0.2-mile stretch of FR 211218. **Trailhead GPS:** N44 43.185' / W107 23.180'

THE HIKE

Trail 001 begins at the closed gate of FR 211218 off of FR 16. Expect to see more elk tracks than people tracks on this trail. Losing elevation steadily, the trail heads east through a patchwork of logging sites.

Black Mountain's forested slope stands to the north, with Black Mountain Lookout Tower (Hike 38) perched atop the rock outcropping cresting above. Views down the Wolf Creek Valley and out to the eastern prairies beyond reveal themselves as well.

Hermit Thrush calls might keep company through the woods as the trail downsizes smaller and smaller from a logging road, to a two-track, and eventually to a single lane. Look for snowshoe hare watching silently with alert eyes.

The trail drops some 800 feet in the final 1.5 miles to reach Quartz Creek. Here the trail shows signs of heavy horse traffic as it travels amongst lodgepole pine forests with a heavy understory of grouse whortleberry, a huckleberry relative of the blueberry.

Big Mountain rises up from the opposite shore at the confluence of Quartz and Wolf Creeks. Wolf Creek joins Quartz Creek from the west and the waters merge taking on the smaller tributary's name, flowing together northward as Wolf Creek. Just south of this confluence, you can hike past an outfitter's picnic grounds to get to the Quartz Creek crossing.

Crossing to the eastern shore of Quartz Creek brings you to the intersection with the Walker Prairie Trail (Trail 014, Hike 33). Walker Prairie Trail crosses the fence line and climbs midway up the grassy slopes of Big Mountain before cruising along southward toward Little and Walker Mountains.

If continuing onward along the Wolf Creek Trail, head left (north) after the crossing to quickly cross back over the creek. As noted earlier, the smaller Wolf Creek merges with Quartz Creek and becomes the namesake body of water at this confluence.

A short bushwhack on the west bank can take you over the smaller Wolf Creek tributary. This will keep your feet dry. But make sure you don't end up heading northwest through the timber on Trail 186 though. You'll find Trail 001 in the meadow at the water's edge.

Just north of this confluence of Quartz and Wolf Creeks, reached either by a double crossing or a short bushwhack, you'll see Trail 001 continuing north through a grassy field. Trail 186 splits off here, heading northwest into the woods, eventually reaching primitive FR 186.

The trail drifts away from the creek bottom and gains elevation along the hillside west of Wolf Creek. After about a mile, the trail reaches the junction with the unmarked post marking the Wolf Creek Falls overlook trail (Hike 35). The Falls Trail heads down to Wolf Creek, while the Wolf Creek Trail continues along the upland slopes.

Trail 001 keeps heading north, rounding the hilltop and dropping down to the trickle of water known as Bear Creek. A trail leads to some corrals and an outfitter camp off to the left, while the main trail keeps right, paralleling Bear Creek.

In June, the conditions are right for an impressive crop of balsamroot, which look like fields of sunflowers. Sprinkled in you'll see lavender lupines, pink geraniums, and azure bluebells. The eastern views continue to impress. Look beyond Big Mountain and Elephant Foot to see the Wyoming prairie through the Wolf Creek Valley.

Less than a mile beyond Bear Creek, the Wolf Creek Trail reaches the intersection with the Horseshoe Mountain Trail (Trail 005, Hike 36) at Sibley Creek. The Horseshoe Mountain Trail heads left (west), while Wolf Creek Trail goes right (east).

After a slight rise coming out of the creek bottom, the Wolf Creek Trail maintains its downward trajectory. Continue following the valley eastward, soaking up the ever more impressive view. The trail is mostly visible in the open meadows, but at times, it fades away. Occasionally it is obscured by multiple cattle and game trails.

Here along the eastern foothills, the geologic folds of the mountain strata are impressive. The cascades and pools of Wolf Creek are equally as impressive. A couple of miles beyond the Sibley Creek crossing, the trail reaches the intersection with the Alden Creek Trail (Trail 072), which ventures off to the south. The main trail continues along Wolf Creek for another mile before reaching the Bighorn National Forest boundary. Beyond this, the trail continues over private land for a mile. Contact the Bighorn National Forest for current access information.

Wolf Creek Trail

Wolf Creek and
Big Mountain

Big Mountain

MILES AND DIRECTIONS

0.0 Trail starts at the gate of FR 211218.

5.4 Trail reaches the confluence of Quartz and Wolf Creeks and the northern end of Walker Prairie Trail (Hike 33).

6.4 Junction with Wolf Falls Trail (Hike 35). Continue straight.

6.9 Ford Bear Creek.

7.6 Cross Sibley Creek to reach the junction with Horseshoe Mountain Trail (Hike 36). Bear right.

9.7 Junction with Alden Creek Trail.

10.6 Bighorn National Forest Boundary. Private property ahead.

11.6 Eatons' Ranch.

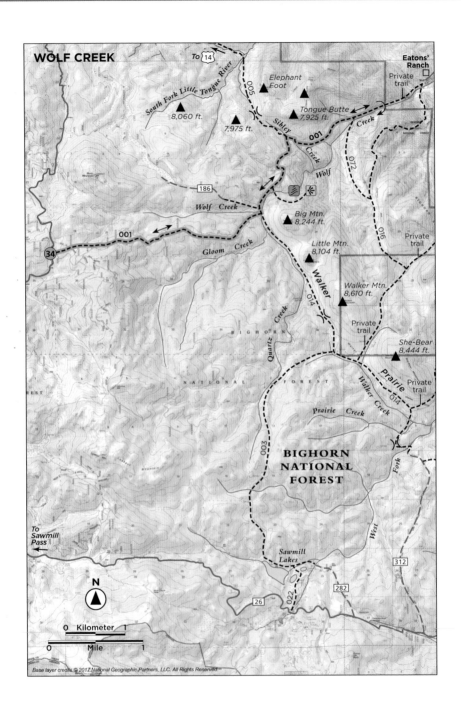

WOLF CREEK

To 14

Eatons' Ranch

Private trail

Elephant Foot

South Fork Little Tongue River

005

Sibley

Tongue Butte 7,925 ft.

Creek

8,060 ft.

001

072

7,975 ft.

Wolf

186

016

Wolf Creek

Big Mtn. 8,244 ft.

Private trail

001

Little Mtn. 8,104 ft.

34

Gloom Creek

Walker

014

Walker Mtn. 8,610 ft.

Private trail

Quartz Creek

She-Bear 8,444 ft.

BIGHORN

Private trail

NATIONAL

FOREST

Prairie

Walker Creek

014

200

Prairie Creek

BIGHORN NATIONAL FOREST

Fork

West

To Sawmill Pass

Sawmill Lakes

312

022

282

N

26

0 Kilometer 1

0 Mile 1

35. **WOLF CREEK FALLS OVERLOOK**

WHY GO?

This short but intense side trip from the Wolf Creek Trail is mostly used by horseback riders from nearby guest ranches. It provides a nice, albeit distant, view of impressive Wolf Creek Falls tumbling down the canyon.

THE RUNDOWN

Distance: 2.6 miles out-and-back extension

Elevation gain: 600 feet

Difficulty: Moderate due to steep climbs, uneven footing, and distance from trailheads

Hiking time: About 1.5 hours

Best seasons: Late spring, summer, early fall

Fees and permits: No fees or permits required

Trail contacts: Bighorn National Forest, 2013 Eastside 2nd St., Sheridan, WY 82801, (307) 674-2600, http://www.fs.usda.gov/bighorn

Maps: USDA Forest Service Bighorn National Forest, USGS Walker Mountain

Dog-friendly: Dogs must be under control

Trail surface: Uneven terrain including heavy rutting

Nearest town: Dayton or Big Horn, Wyoming

Other trail users: Equestrians

Special considerations: Wolf Creek Falls Overlook is accessed off of the Wolf Creek Trail (Trail 001, Hike 34). Trail 001 can be reached from Steamboat Point via Trail 005 (Hike 36) in the north or off of FR 16 from the west. From the east, the Wolf Creek Trail crosses private property before reaching the Bighorn National Forest Boundary. Eatons' Guest Ranch generously provides limited access to the trail, but access can be restricted seasonally. Contact the Bighorn National Forest to determine current access.

FINDING THE TRAILHEAD

This is a side trail off of the Wolf Creek Trail (Hike 34).
Trailhead GPS: N44 44.502' / W107 18.045'

THE HIKE

The Wolf Creek Falls Overlook Trail isn't marked on the maps, but it is a well-worn path. It takes off from an unmarked post at an intersection in a clearing

Wolf Falls

Grouse whortleberry is an abundant understory plant in the Bighorns, including along the Wolf Falls Trail.

above Wolf Creek, about a mile north of the confluence of Wolf and Quartz Creeks (see Hike 34). The trail enters the woods and quickly bottoms out at Wolf Creek. Looking downstream, it is hard to believe that such an epic falls is just a short distance away. After crossing the creek, head downstream through the meadow to pick up the trail again as it enters the trees.

An intense climb gains back that elevation you just dropped. This time you're climbing the forested slopes of Big Mountain. After hoofing up this myself, I understand why most folks use horses to get here. The Christmas Trail peels off to the right, while the Wolf Creek Falls Overlook Trail keeps left. From here, you'll once again drop elevation at a steady clip.

The trail is less evident as it drifts toward the Wolf Creek drainage far below. You'll hear the falls before the trees thin out enough to give you a view. Scrambling up a boulder might help give you the extra few feet of height to get a less obstructed view. The forested slopes and the craggy rock face make for a nice contrast of landscapes surrounding the falls.

Retrace your steps to return to the Wolf Creek Trail.

MILES AND DIRECTIONS

0.0   Junction with Wolf Creek Trail.

0.3   Trail fords Wolf Creek.

0.6   Junction with Christmas Trail. Keep left.

1.3   Wolf Falls overlook.

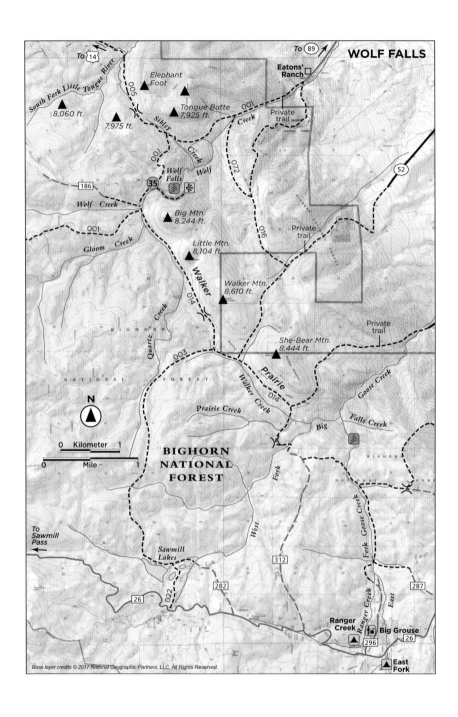

WOLF FALLS

To 14

To 89

Eatons' Ranch

South Fork Little Tongue River

Elephant Foot

Tongue Butte
7,925 ft.

8,060 ft.

7,975 ft.

005

Sibley Creek

001

Private trail

52

101

Creek

072

Wolf Falls

Wolf

186

35

Wolf   Creek

Big Mtn.
8,244 ft.

016

Private trail

001

Gloom   Creek

Little Mtn.
8,104 ft

Walker

014

Walker Mtn.
8,610 ft.

Private trail

BIGHORN

Quartz   Creek

003

She-Bear Mtn.
8,444 ft.

NATIONAL   FOREST

Walker   Creek

Prairie

014

Goose Creek

N

Prairie Creek

Big

Falls Creek

BIGHOR

0   Kilometer   1

0   Mile   1

BIGHORN NATIONAL FOREST

NATIONAL   FORE

West

Fork

312

Fork Goose Creek

287

To Sawmill Pass

Sawmill Lakes

022

282

26

Ranger Creek

296

Ranger Creek

East

26

Big Grouse

East Fork

36. HORSESHOE MOUNTAIN, TRAIL 005

WHY GO?

An easily accessible hike right off of US Hwy. 14, the Horseshoe Mountain Trail explores the scenic grassland meadows on the western side of iconic Horseshoe Mountain west of Dayton. This hike can provide a route to the Wolf Creek Falls (Hike 35) or into the northern stretches of Walker Prairie (Hike 33) via a short segment of the Wolf Creek Trail (Hike 34).

THE RUNDOWN

Distance: 5.8 miles one-way circuit or 11.6 miles round trip out-and-back

Elevation gain: 1,430 feet

Difficulty: Moderate due to elevation gains, distance, and uneven footing

Hiking time: About 3 miles

Best seasons: Late spring, summer, early fall

Fees and permits: No fees or permits required

Trail contacts: Bighorn National Forest, 2013 Eastside 2nd St., Sheridan, WY 82801, (307) 674-2600, http://www.fs.usda.gov/bighorn

Maps: USDA Forest Service Bighorn National Forest, USGS Dayton South

Dog-friendly: Dogs must be under control

Trail surface: Uneven terrain

Nearest town: Dayton, Wyoming

Other trail users: None

FINDING THE TRAILHEAD

 From Dayton, follow US Hwy. 14 west for almost 13 miles. A large parking lot is on the north side of the highway at the base of Steamboat Point. The trail is on the south side of the highway, opposite the parking area.
Trailhead GPS: N44 48.129' / W107 21.880'

THE HIKE

The eastern slopes of Horseshoe Mountain are visible from US Hwy. 14 west of Dayton. Countless folks turn into the pullouts, snap a few photos, and then hurry along on their way deep into the mountains. The jumble of rock that makes up Fallen City is plenty cool, but I'd argue that the grassland scenes on the backside of Horseshoe Mountain are far more impressive. The exposed reefs of Steamboat

Point, Horseshoe Mountain, and Elephant Foot are unique features to behold. Add this to a ribbon of grassland meadows, a swath of mountain forests, and some of the prettiest waters around, and you've got the fixings for a memorable and photogenic hike. The drawback to all of this is the same steep grades that slow the big rigs down on the highway. You'll have to tackle those inclines on foot.

Start by parking in the lot beneath Steamboat Point. Next, look both ways, and then cross to the south side of the highway. The trail (Trail 005) follows an old rutted two-track down to the bottom of the draw, 0.6 mile below. Cross the Little Tongue River, a knee-high ford, and head south (through the trees) and up a steep incline. A quarter of a mile into the climb, you'll transition from the trees to a grassy field. You'll also cross through the first gate. This serves as a reminder that the area is grazed during the summer months. Please leave gates as you find them.

Enjoy the views of exposed ridge along Horseshoe Mountain and a perspective on Fallen City that few see. You'll cross another fence line in 0.8 mile. This is along the saddle that divides the Little Tongue River from the South Fork of the Little Tongue. Look back for fine views of Steamboat Point. Also note Trail 427 heads south from here, although it is hard to pick out in the meadow grasses. The main trail continues on to the southeast, soon passing a brass marker from the original Bighorn Forest Reserve, circa 1902. The trail follows the long valley 1.7 miles to another gate. Here the path comes and goes, as you weave down a spring-fed trickle of water, navigating the path of least resistance until you reach the South Fork of the Little Tongue. The South Fork flows northeast circumnavigating Horseshoe Mountain. You should be able to cross it easily.

Elephant Foot along
Horseshoe Mountain Trail

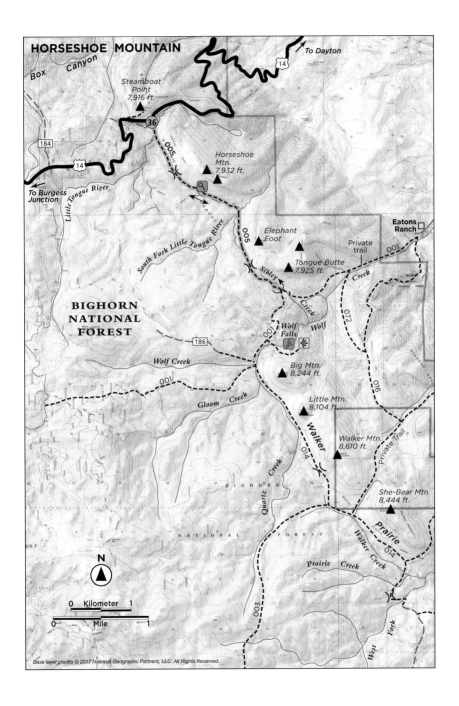

HORSESHOE MOUNTAIN

Box Canyon

To Dayton

14

Steamboat Point
7,916 ft.

184

14

36

005

Horseshoe Mtn.
7,932 ft.

To Burgess Junction

Little Tongue River

South Fork Little Tongue River

005

Elephant Foot

Tongue Butte
7,925 ft.

Eatons Ranch

Private trail

001

Sibley Creek

Creek

Wolf Creek

Wolf Falls

Wolf

072

010

BIGHORN NATIONAL FOREST

001

186

Wolf Creek

Big Mtn.
8,244 ft.

001

Gloom Creek

Little Mtn.
8,104 ft.

Walker

Walker Mtn.
8,610 ft.

Private Trail

014

Quartz Creek

She-Bear Mtn.
8,444 ft.

BIGHORN

NATIONAL FOREST

Prairie

014

Prairie Creek

Walker Creek

West Fork

005

N

0   Kilometer   1

0   Mile   1

Base layer credits © 2017 National Geographic Partners, LLC. All Rights Reserved.

Cattle trails make navigating a bit tricky after the crossing. Trail 005 heads south, mostly staying in the grassy meadow below the face of Elephant Foot, only occasionally working into the edge of the trees to the west. There is another gate a quarter of a mile after the crossing. Keep heading up the drainage. A little over 1 mile past the crossing, Trail 426 heads off to the northeast. Stick to the main trail to pass the grazing exclosure, eventually cresting the divide, and then dropping into the valley of Sibley Creek.

Again, the trail is a network of paths along both banks of the faint watercourse. About a mile, say two-thirds the way down the valley or so, the Horseshoe Mountain Trail ends as it bisects the Wolf Creek Trail at an obvious water crossing.

MILES AND DIRECTIONS

0.0   Parking lot at the base of Steamboat Point.

0.6   Little Tongue River crossing.

1.7   Trail crosses a divide to enter South Fork of Little Tongue drainage.

3.4   Trail fords South Fork of Little Tongue River

4.7   Trail crosses the pass to enter Wolf Creek watershed.

5.8   Junction with Wolf Creek Trail.

37. STEAMBOAT POINT, TRAIL 630

WHY GO?

A beacon right off of US Hwy. 14, the climb to the top of Steamboat Point tests the lungs and the calves, but the rewards are stunning views. It is a short enough hike that even younger explores can make the trip.

THE RUNDOWN

Distance: 1.4 miles out-and-back

Elevation gain: 665 feet

Difficulty: Moderate due to uneven footing, steep inclines, and exposed hiking

Hiking time: About 1 hour

Best seasons: Spring and fall

Fees and permits: No fees or permits required

Trail contacts: Bighorn National Forest, 2013 Eastside 2nd St., Sheridan, WY 82801, (307)

674-2600, http://www.fs.usda.gov/bighorn

Maps: USDA Forest Service Bighorn National Forest, USGS Dayton South

Dog-friendly: Dogs must be under control

Trail surface: Uneven terrain

Nearest town: Dayton, Wyoming

Other trail users: None

Special considerations: No water available

FINDING THE TRAILHEAD

From Dayton, follow US Hwy. 14 west for almost 13 miles. A large parking lot is on the north side of the highway at the base of Steamboat Point. The trail is on the south side of the highway, opposite the parking area.

Trailhead GPS: N44 48.192' / W107 21.906'

THE HIKE

Parking is right off of US Hwy. 14, so this makes a convenient day trip just west of Dayton.

Steamboat Point is a prominent feature seen from the highway, and it is one of those hikes that folks should do just because they can. In fact, I've seen a busload of elementary school aged kids tackle this feat for just that reason.

The route up to the base of the rocky cliff is the visible track. From here, the trail wraps around the southeastern flank of the mountain. Next, the trail follows a gap in the rocks as it winds steadily through a steep slot via a series of switchbacks. The trail tops out on the flattop surface of Steamboat Point amid sparse woodlands of whitebark and limber pines.

The views to the east seem to go on for forever from Steamboat Point as you gaze across the northern Wyoming prairies. The lookout tower on Black Mountain is visible from here, as are the tallest peaks of the Cloud Peak Wilderness. To the north is the valley of the Tongue River as it emerges from the granite slit of Box Canyon.

MILES AND DIRECTIONS

0.0   Trailhead.

0.7   Summit of Steamboat Point.

Narrow trail along Steamboat Point
CHARLES HUBBELL

Looking east from
Steamboat Point Trail
CHARLES HUBBELL

Steamboat Point views
CHARLES HUBBELL

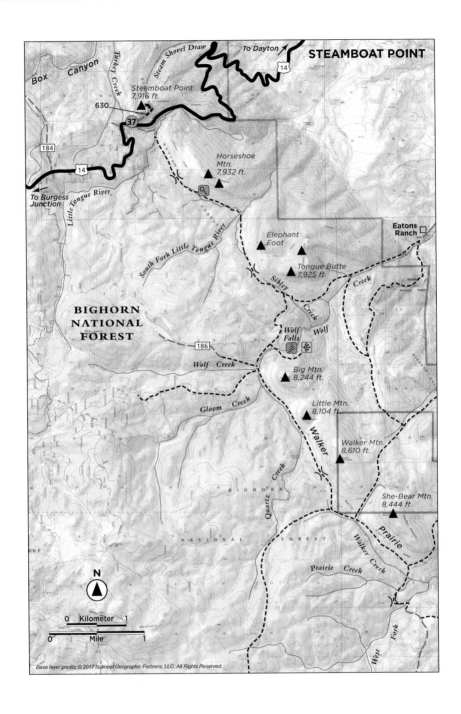

STEAMBOAT POINT

38. BLACK MOUNTAIN LOOKOUT, TRAIL 011

WHY GO?

As to be expected from a hike to a lookout tower, this trail goes up, up, and more up. Hikers gain nearly 1,300 feet elevation in a mere 1.2 miles. The rocky crags at the top of Black Mountain are neat, and the stunning panoramic views will occupy you for long enough to catch your breath before the return trip down, down, and more down.

THE RUNDOWN

Distance: 2.4 miles out-and-back

Elevation gain: 1,269 feet

Difficulty: Moderate due to steep inclines and uneven terrain

Hiking time: About 1.5 hours

Best seasons: Spring, summer, fall

Fees and permits: No fees or permits required

Trail contacts: Bighorn National Forest, 2013 Eastside 2nd St., Sheridan, WY 82801, (307) 674-2600, http://www.fs.usda.gov/bighorn

Maps: USDA Forest Service Bighorn National Forest, USGS Woodrock

Dog-friendly: Dogs must be under control

Trail surface: Uneven terrain with lots of rocks near top

Nearest town: Dayton, Wyoming

Other trail users: None

Special considerations: No water available

FINDING THE TRAILHEAD

Take US Hwy. 14 to FR 16 between Dayton and Burgess Junction. Despite some major potholes, FR 16 is a solid road, although the side roads off of it can be a bit dicey. Head south on FR 16 for 3.5 miles. Turn left (east) onto FR 222. The trailhead is 1 mile down this road, although, depending on your vehicle, you might have to park before you reach the end of the road.
Trailhead GPS: N44 44.261' / W107 23.206'

THE HIKE

From the end of the road to the lookout tower is probably a half a mile as the crow flies. But since you aren't a crow, the hike is about 1.2 miles each way. You'll gain

Black Mountain Lookout

1,269 feet elevation, but the bright side is it's downhill on the way back. The views from the top make the grueling mile well worth it.

Initially, you'll continue southeast at the end of the road. After about a half a mile, the trail bends back to the northwest. This is the first in a series of switchbacks, each getting progressively tighter than the last. Most of the hike is through stands of lodgepole pine. See if you can find any signs of the historic fire that consumed much of the vegetation along this slope. The final push is a scramble up the 9,489-foot granite knob of Black Mountain. It's a bit rocky. Don't let the incredible views distract you, watch your step.

Once you reach the top, take in the view of the high peaks to the south. The jagged peak, Black Tooth Mountain, is the namesake for a favorite local brewery. The panoramic views east are unobstructed for miles.

This is one of three lookout towers that remain in the Bighorns. Sheep Mountain and High Point Lookout Towers are off of US Hwy. 16 just east and west of Powder River Pass, respectively. Sheep Mountain Lookout is available for overnight rentals through the Forest Service. James T. Saban Lookout is a short day hike (Hike 10).

Clark's Nutcracker

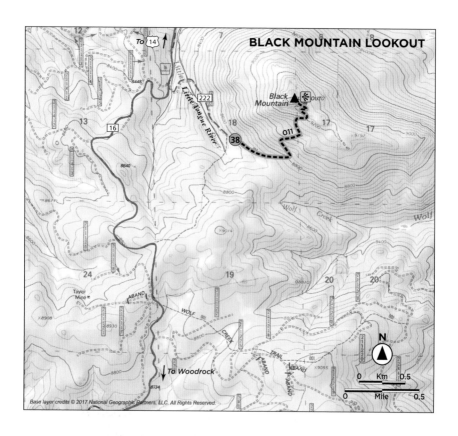

MILES AND DIRECTIONS

0.0   Trailhead.

1.2   Black Mountain Lookout.

39. TONGUE RIVER CANYON, TRAIL 002

WHY GO?

The Tongue River has carved out an impressive canyon, and with some navigational skills, hikers can follow the trail from the trailhead just west of Dayton, all the way to the Burgess Junction area. Or you could reverse it for a more downhill jaunt.

THE RUNDOWN

Distance: 9.1 miles one-way, point-to-point or out-and-back

Elevation gain: 3,280 feet

Difficulty: Moderate to cave, strenuous to FR 196 due to distance and elevation gains

Hiking time: About 1 hour for cave, about 7 hours for trail

Best seasons: Spring fall

Fees and permits: No fees or permits required

Trail contacts: Bighorn National Forest, 2013 Eastside 2nd St., Sheridan, WY 82801, (307)

674-2600, http://www.fs.usda.gov/bighorn

Maps: USDA Forest Service Bighorn National Forest, USGS Dayton South, USGS Skull Ridge

Dog-friendly: Dogs must be under control

Trail surface: Uneven terrain

Nearest town: Dayton, Wyoming

Other trail users: None

Special considerations: The Bighorn Mountain Wild and Scenic Trail Run uses this trail in mid-June.

FINDING THE TRAILHEAD

From the east end of Dayton, just east of the bridge crossing the Tongue River, take River Road (Sheridan County Rd. 92) north and then west along the Tongue River. After 2 miles, the road splits. Keep left, following the narrow potholed road into the head of the Tongue River Canyon. The road dead ends at the Amsden Creek Wildlife Habitat Management Area.
Trailhead GPS: N44 50.820' / W107 19.809'

THE HIKE

Like the Little Horn Trail (Hike 41), this trail sees heavy use during the Bighorn Mountain Trail Run in June. Unlike the Little Horn Trail, it also sees heavy use for the rest of the year. The majority of folks take the short leg up the sidewall to

Tongue River

visit the cave. Or they are fishing this renowned stretch of trout water. The farther you travel from the parking lot, the fewer folks you will find.

The Tongue River Canyon Trail (Trail 002) takes off from the parking lot of the Amsden Creek Wildlife Habitat Management Area. It follows the northern bank of the Tongue River as it passes through a deep and rugged gorge. Cliffs rise overhead providing nesting ledges for raptors. A small arch is visible down the canyon.

After a quarter of a mile, a solid bridge provides a crossing to the trail for Tongue River Cave. This short side trip scales up the steep hillside, reaching an impressive cave. The graffiti detracts from the experience, but the cool cave air is a refreshing relief after the intense climb. Bring a flashlight if you plan on entering the cave. The natural light from outside gets you only as far as the first ledge. True spelunkers have mapped over a mile of passages here, but most folks should stick to the first large cavern room.

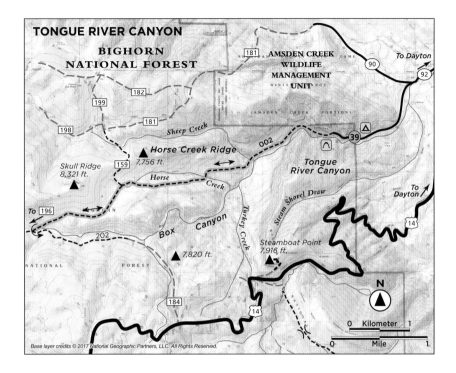

If you are skipping the cave detour, instead of crossing the bridge, you'll simply continue westward along the northern bank of the Tongue River. The hike is awe-inspiring, and you'll find it slow-going as you stop to take landscape pictures from every angle. The riparian ribbon of Cottonwood and Box Elder trees follows the course of the river. Ponderosa pines grow thicker here, and massive limestone boulders litter the landscape at random.

After 2 miles, and just shy of 1,000 vertical feet up, the trail enters into vast meadows. The views become even more impressive as the mountain peaks fill the sky above and the canyon funnels the view below. Here the trail drops down to cross Sheep Creek. You might want to top off your water bottles here. Like everywhere in the Bighorns, purifying is always recommended.

Peering over the edge of Box Canyon offers up another side exploration, or the main trail climbs the steep hillside for the next 2.5 miles. With each step up, the immenseness of the landscape is undeniable. This grassy slope provides summer pasture for cattle and critical winter range for elk herds.

You're pushing 5 miles from the trailhead when you cross Horse Creek. After the crossing, you continue to climb for another mile, keeping to the south of Horse Creek, with its namesake ridge paralleling to the north. Then you cross back over to the north bank. Here, ATV Trail 159 heads more northerly through the gate, while the footpath veers southwest. The trail fades in and out, crosses Horse Creek again, and, generally aims for the pass.

Beyond this dip, you shoot for the intersection of the South Fork of the Tongue entering the main river drainage. Follow the maze of trails down the final 1.5 miles. Fishing trails follow the shores. The official trail crosses the Tongue River just west of the confluence and continues a steep climb westward. The trail ends at primitive FR 196.

MILES AND DIRECTIONS

0.0   Trailhead at Amsden Creek Wildlife Habitat Management Area.

0.2   Bridge leads to Tongue River Cave. Continue straight.

2.1   Head of Tongue River Canyon.

2.2   Trail crosses Sheep Creek.

3.4   Trail crosses Horse Creek.

5.0   Trail crosses Horse Creek again.

7.3   Reach a gate along an unnamed pass.

9.1   Tongue River near FR 196.

NORTHEAST BIGHORNS ADDITIONAL HIKES

Cutler Hill Nordic Ski Trail (Trail 552) offers skiing on gentle slopes, spur trails, and a meadow loop. Dogs are allowed here even in winter. Trails can be a bit soggy in summer.

Sibley Lake Nordic Ski Trail (Trail 558) is a network of groomed trails for classic and skate skiing in the winter. In summer, hikers use the area but the trails travel through some wet areas. Dogs are not permitted in winter.

Prune Creek Trail (Trail 013) is a short trail within the Sibley Nordic Trail system. Anglers mostly use it during the warmer seasons.

The Soldier Ridge Trail is about a 5-minute drive from downtown Sheridan, just past where the pavement turns to gravel on West 5th St. Take the second left, cross the cattle guard, and then turn right into the parking lot. This 4-mile trail offers stunning views of the Bighorn Mountains. This is a private property easement administered by the Sheridan Community Land Trust. Please respect the landowners and the rules.

MEDICINE WHEEL AND SURROUNDINGS

The northern end of the Bighorn Mountains has long been a sacred land. This high and windswept region is home to the Medicine Wheel Historic Site. The massive stone structure is important in religious ceremonies and has astronomical connections.

Nearby, Bucking Mule Falls represents the only National Recreation Trail in the Bighorn Mountains. While Porcupine Falls plummets 200 feet, and the hike drops over twice as far to take in the view.

Bull Elk Park represents unique grasslands more typically found far to the west in eastern Washington.

The Little Horn Trail connects northeastern rangelands to the mountains, while Cottonwood Canyon is a major canyon flanking the western slopes of the Bighorns and badlands of the Bighorn Basin.

The Medicine Wheel Scenic Passage, US Hwy. Alternate 14, travels from Burgess Junction west to Lovell. This route is closed in the winter.

Northwestern Bighorns near Medicine Mountain and Bucking Mule Falls National Recreation Trail

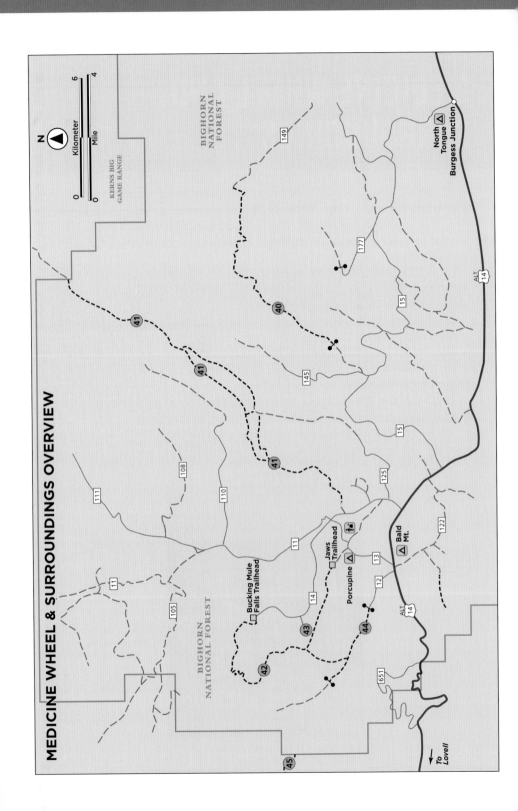

40. **BULL ELK PARK, TRAIL 076**

WHY GO?
Bull Elk Park is uniquely situated in the northern Bighorn Mountains. Dominated by Idaho fescue and bluebunch wheatgrass, Bull Elk Park is a disjunct of Palouse Prairie far more representative of the eastern Washington grasslands.

THE RUNDOWN

Distance: 10.4 miles out-and-back

Elevation gain: 2,100 feet

Difficulty: Moderate due to distance and elevation on return hike

Hiking time: About 5 hours

Best seasons: Summer fall

Fees and permits: No fees or permits required

Trail contacts: Bighorn National Forest, 2013 Eastside 2nd St., Sheridan, WY 82801, (307)

674-2600, http://www.fs.usda.gov/bighorn

Maps: USDA Forest Service Bighorn National Forest, USGS Bull Elk Park, USGS Ice Creek

Dog-friendly: Dogs must be under control

Trail surface: Uneven terrain

Nearest town: Dayton, Wyoming

Other trail users: None

Special considerations: None

FINDING THE TRAILHEAD

From US Hwy. Alternate 14 west of Burgess Junction, follow the Dayton Gulch Road (FR 15) northward. Then take FR 145 north, and make an immediate right on FR 147. This primitive road climbs through a saddle and continues up a steep ridge for 1.4 miles to reach a gate. The hike starts here at the closed road.
Trailhead GPS: N44 50.242' / W107 42.107'

THE HIKE
The Bull Elk Park area was recognized by the Forest Service as a Research Natural Area in 1952. As such, livestock grazing is not allowed here. The hike can be a day-hike destination, or it makes for a pleasant backpacking trip.

The initial leg of this hike follows a closed jeep trail down the ridgetop, eventually reaching the vast meadows of Bull Elk Park. Beyond this, the trail is difficult to locate, although adventurers might take joy in pushing onward to reach the bottom of Dry Fork of the Little Bighorn River after an insanely steep pitch of blocky cliffs guarding the river.

Look for red squirrels throughout the Bighorns, especially along the Bull Elk Park Trail

The former road provides easy walking as the trail ventures down the ridge-line. Trees have returned to areas that were logged here decades ago. Gaps in the canopy offer occasional views of Lick Creek to the southeast and Bear Trap Creek to the northwest. After reaching a large ridgetop meadow, the elevation continues to drop at a gradual pace.

The trail eventually exits the timber and enters the southwestern arm of Bull Elk Park. Continue into the park, keeping an eye out for wildlife. Fisher Mountain dominates the northern views, while Dry Fork Ridge stands to northeast. By following the treeline along the southeast cove of Bull Elk Park, you can find a

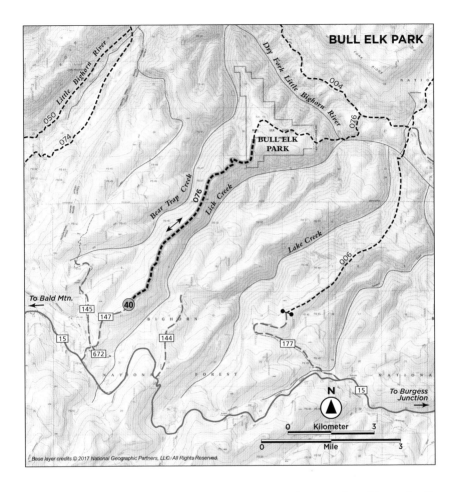

well-worn trail through the woods and into a small clearing. This additional mile leads to an outfitters camp and a spring on the far edge of this meadow.

Maps show the trail continuing on eastward, eventually crossing Lick Creek near its intersection with the Dry Fork of the Little Bighorn. With some navigational skills, this would be possible; however, don't count on a distinct trail to show you the way.

MILES AND DIRECTIONS

0.0   Trailhead. Hike down closed road.

4.7   Trail enters Bull Elk Park Research Natural Area.

5.2   Trail enters Bull Elk Park.

41. **LITTLE HORN TRAIL, TRAIL 050**

WHY GO?

This route takes hikers from the spruce-lined mountains to the ponderosa pine bottoms of the Little Bighorn River, dropping nearly 5,000 feet in elevation along the way. The lower section of the trail is accessed from Kerns Wildlife Habitat Management Area and can provide top-notch trout fishing.

THE RUNDOWN

Distance: 16.3 miles one-way, point-to-point or out-and-back

Elevation gain: 4,870 feet

Difficulty: Strenuous due to length and elevation change

Hiking time: About 11 hours

Best seasons: Summer fall

Fees and permits: No fees or permits required

Trail contacts: Bighorn National Forest, 2013 Eastside 2nd St., Sheridan, WY 82801, (307) 674-2600, http://www.fs.usda.gov/bighorn Wyoming Game & Fish

Maps: USDA Forest Service Bighorn National Forest, USGS

Bull Elk Park, USGS Boyd Ridge, USGS Bald Mountain

Dog-friendly: Dogs must be under control

Trail surface: Uneven terrain

Nearest town: Ranchester, Wyoming or Wyola, Montana

Other trail users: Equestrians

Special considerations: Kerns Wildlife Management Area is closed each year to vehicles Nov 1–May 31 and to human presence Nov 16–May 31. Also keep in mind that the Bighorn Mountain Wild and Scenic Trail Run uses this trail in mid-June.

FINDING THE TRAILHEAD

Drive northwest from Ranchester on Wyoming 343 (old US Hwy. 89). After 12 miles, turn left (west) onto Sheridan County Rd. 144, following it for 16.5 miles. Upon reaching the bottoms of the Little Bighorn River, the county road bends eastward. (This spot can also be reached from Wyola, Montana along Country Rd. 418.) Turn left (west) onto a primitive road that is marked "public access through private lands" which crosses briefly into Montana. This road is rough with some fords, and high clearance is required. Follow it for 2.8 miles to park at the trailhead on the Kerns Wildlife Management Unit. Hike the road to reach the beginning of the trail.

To reach the upper trailhead, take US Hwy. Alternate 14 west from Burgess Junction to reach FR 14. Follow it for 2.5 miles. Parking is on the right, just

beyond FR 135. The sign reads "Little Bighorn Trail," but locally the trail is referred to as the Little Horn Trail.
Trailhead GPS: N44 58.803' / W107 38.859'

THE HIKE

Most of the time you're likely to have this trail all to yourself. It is a main artery for the annual Bighorn Mountain Trail Run, though, so for one weekend in June, you can expect to share it with a couple hundred elite athletes. They make the trails look far easier than they actually are.

The journey to this remote trailhead is an adventure in and of itself, crossing briefly into Montana and the Crow Reservation and then traveling along a rough and private access road, crossing back into Wyoming along the route.

The hike begins by passing Wyoming Game and Fish's Little Horn Patrol Cabin as well as several private structures. A combination of ponderosa pine and Douglas-fir shade the area. The Dry Fork Ridge Trail (Trail 004) heads left, over the bridge and up the hill. The Little Horn Trail keeps to the north side of the Little Bighorn River, a fast and cool stream noted for its fishing.

The steep slopes of Fisher Mountain quickly become visible, as the rocky path parallels the river. Crossing a stretch of open country, the Boyd Ridge Trail (Trail 096) soon splits off to the right. The Little Horn Trail continues up the broad valley.

The trail then returns to the riverbank, following it into an inner gorge of ancient granite. Passing a waterfall, the trail zigzags up the base of the cliffs, charting an unlikely course along the high ledges. Then it descends to reach the bottomlands beyond the gorge.

From here, after following the river for a short bit, the trail swings upward across open grasslands sprinkled with scattered pockets of ponderosa pine and Douglas-fir. Now rising well above the river, the trail works through the woods and past a cliff-lined portal of the Dry Fork of the Little Bighorn.

Steep slopes and cutbanks limit access to the river between Dry Fork and Taylor Creek. Trail 074 does make a crossing of the Little Bighorn River just above its confluence with Taylor Creek, however. Trail 074, the "Taylor Stock Creek Driveway" or the Fuller Trail, travels south of the Little Bighorn River, reconnecting with the Little Horn Trail via FR 125.

The Little Horn Trail keeps on the north side of the river here, traveling southwest past grassy meadows and brushfields. The sedimentary walls of Boyd Ridge tower overhead, and soon the gushing waterfalls of Leaky Mountain can be seen. The unique falls seep through subterranean passageways before springing from the limestone cliffs.

After crossing the stream flowing from Leaky Mountain, the trail initiates a steady climb across rolling country, climbing saddle after saddle. Enjoy the final views of Little Bighorn Canyon behind you as you push onward.

At the top of the grade, sagebrush flats sit high above the merging of Wagon Box Creek and the Little Bighorn River. An expansive prairie sits ahead. It's possible to cut south and pick up the end of FR 125 and Trail 074 here. Trail 050 stays high on the grassy balds to the north of Wagon Box Creek.

Fisher Mountain and Little Horn Trail

Little Bighorn River

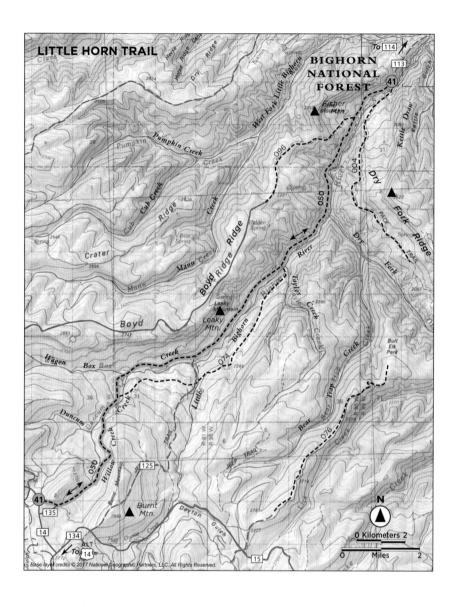

After a mile and a half or so, Duncum Creek enters from the south. Cross Wagon Box Creek just above the confluence. The route climbs through sagebrush heading westward, ultimately leveling off and turning south.

The final 3 miles of trail continue to pick up elevation, as it fords Duncum Creek and then makes multiple crossings of Willow Creek. Bald topped Burnt Mountain rises to the east. The ecological process of succession is evident as you cross through a portion of the 1978 Half Ounce burn. Beyond this, the trail turns west for the final ascent to the upper trailhead. At the top of the grade, shoot across an open meadow, cross through a gate, and reach the well-marked parking area just off of FR 14.

MILES AND DIRECTIONS

0.0   Trailhead in Kerns Wildlife Management Unit. Hike west along road.

0.2   Road ends. Bear right as trail follows north bank of Little Bighorn River.

1.7   Junction with Boyd Ridge Trail. Continue straight ahead.

2.1   Granite inner gorge of Little Bighorn Canyon.

6.2   Junction with Fuller Trail ("Taylor Creek Stock Driveway"). Continue straight ahead.

7.4   Trail crosses stream that issues from Leaky Mountain.

9.7   Confluence of Little Bighorn and Wagon Box Creek. Trail continues southwest along Wagon Box.

11.4   Trail fords Wagon Box Creek.

12.2   Upper junction with Fuller Trail. Keep right.

13.2   Trail fords Duncum Creek.

13.6   First of Willow Creek fords.

14.5   Final ford of Willow Creek. Trail begins final ascent.

16.3   Trail reaches trailhead just off FR 14.

42. BUCKING MULE FALLS, TRAIL 053

WHY GO?

This is the only National Recreation Trail designated in the Bighorns. The majority of users make the 5-mile round trip to the Bucking Mule Falls Overlook. The trail continues on, crossing through the upper reaches of Devil Canyon ending at Jaws Trailhead.

THE RUNDOWN

Distance: 13.5 miles one-way, point-to-point or out-and-back

Elevation gain: 2,425 feet

Difficulty: Moderate to falls, strenuous overall due to length and elevation changes with steep inclines

Hiking time: About 2 hours for falls, about 12 hours for trail

Best seasons: Summer early fall

Fees and permits: No fees or permits required

Trail contacts: Bighorn National Forest, 2013 Eastside 2nd St., Sheridan, WY 82801, (307)

674-2600, http://www.fs.usda.gov/bighorn

Maps: USDA Forest Service Bighorn National Forest, USGS Mexican Hill, USGS Bald Mountain, and USGS Medicine Wheel

Dog-friendly: Dogs must be under control

Trail surface: Uneven terrain

Nearest town: Lovell, Wyoming

Other trail users: Equestrians

Special considerations: Scheduled for minor rerouting in the coming years

FINDING THE TRAILHEAD

 Take US Hwy. Alternate 14 west from Burgess Junction to reach FR 14. Follow FR 14 for 3 miles. Bear left at the junction with FR 11 to stay on FR 14. Follow FR 14 for another 8 miles to reach Bucking Mule Falls Trailhead. The southern end of the trail can be accessed from the Jaws Trailhead, along FR 133, which connects FR 13 with FR 14 and 11.

Trailhead GPS: N44 53.040' / W107 54.393'

THE HIKE

This National Recreation Trail makes for a great day hike to the Bucking Mule Falls overlook, or an ambitious backpacking adventure through rugged Devil Canyon. This route is popular with horseback riders.

The walk to the falls overlook is an easy day hike. The full Bucking Mule Falls National Recreation Trail trip is more intense, thanks to impressive climbs down, and then back up steep canyon walls. Overall, you lose and then regain over 3,000 feet in elevation.

Initially the trail skirts Bucking Mule Canyon before taking the plunge deep into Devil Canyon. Along the way, take in views of Mexican Hill across the Porcupine Creek valley. A bridge crosses over Big Teepee Creek. The spur trail to Bucking Mule Falls overlook is at a well-marked junction. The overlook is perched high atop a granite spur, and you get that edge of the world feeling if you approach too close to the rim. The Bucking Mule Falls tumble some 600 feet, with peak flows as the snow melts in early summer. The access road can be covered in snow until June, so be sure to check with Forest Service officials when planning early-season trips.

From the overlook spur, the main trail ventures on. As you approach the rim of Devil Canyon, Porcupine Creek runs some 2,000 feet below. The drop to the bottom of the canyon travels through numerous forest types including lodgepole pine, subalpine fir, and Engelmann spruce. Remember in these parts, pines have packets of needles, firs have flat friendly needles, and spruce have single square needles that are sharp. Douglas-fir, identified by its distinct cone with unique tree tailed bracts

Bucking Mule Falls National
Recreation Trail sign
TARA KUIPERS

occupies drier sites along this trail. Whitebark pine also occurs in limited numbers here. As do some juniper.

The trail makes numerous switchbacks as it drops elevation, and the Forest Service has plans for adding more in the coming years. Shortcutting the bends can cause damage to the environment, so stick to the trail. After the grueling descent, the trail bottoms out at the banks of Porcupine Creek. This spot makes for pleasant camping. Refill your water bottles here before continuing on.

After crossing over Porcupine Creek, the trail starts making the climb up Railroad Ridge. A side trail materializes after a long mile up. The Mexican Hill Trail (Trail 054) climbs a steep pitch to reach FR 141.

After a short burst down the steep slope, the trail crosses several boggy brooks. Then it's back uphill, traveling high above Porcupine Creek. Here the sagebrush terrain offers up spectacular views deep into the heart of Devil Canyon. Then it's

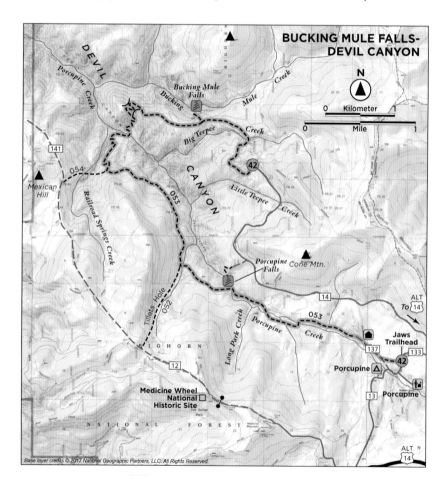

back into the forest, the trail meandering near the canyon edge on occasion for natural overlooks.

Nearly 9 miles in, the trail makes another short descent, this time entering the Tillets Hole Drainage. Another side trail, the rugged and steep Tillets Hole Trail (Trail 052), leads south to FR 12. A mile or so beyond the Tillets Hole Trail, the Bucking Mule Falls trail reunites with Porcupine Creek. After crossing the creek again, the trail climbs the rest of the way out of the canyon, reaching the Jaws Trailhead not far from Porcupine Creek Campground.

MILES AND DIRECTIONS

0.0   Bucking Mule Falls Trailhead.

1.2   Trail crosses Big Teepee Creek.

2.4   Junction with spur trail to falls overlook (0.2 mile, easy); bear left for Devil Canyon.

3.6   Saddle above Devil Canyon.

4.8   Bridge over Porcupine Creek.

5.9   Junction with Railroad Ridge Trail to top of grade. Bear left.

6.4   Devil Canyon viewpoint.

8.9   Trail passes spring and enters Tillets Hole.

9.3   Junction with Tillets Hole Trail. Turn left.

10.5   Bridge leads to east bank of Porcupine Creek.

10.9   Trial passes mouth of Long Park Creek. Continue up east bank.

11.4   Ford of Porcupine Creek.

11.9   Junction with Long Park Creek Trail. Continue straight ahead.

12.1   Cross back to east bank of creek.

12.4   Reach FR 137.

12.7   Trail 053 heads to Jaws Trailhead.

13.5   Jaws Trailhead.

43. PORCUPINE FALLS, TRAIL 135

WHY GO?

In addition to the impressive Porcupine Falls, this steep hike leads to an abandoned mining camp, circa early 1900s.

THE RUNDOWN

Distance: 0.8 mile out-and-back

Elevation gain: 410 feet

Difficulty: Moderate due to steep inclines, elevation gains, multiple steps and uneven footing

Hiking time: About 1 hour

Best seasons: Late spring, summer, fall

Fees and permits: No fees or permits required

Trail contacts: Bighorn National Forest, 2013 Eastside 2nd St., Sheridan, WY 82801, (307) 674-2600, http://www.fs.usda.gov/bighorn

Maps: USDA Forest Service Bighorn National Forest, USGS Medicine Wheel

Dog-friendly: Leashed dogs are permitted

Trail surface: Uneven terrain, uneven steps

Nearest town: Lovell, Wyoming

Other trail users: None

FINDING THE TRAILHEAD

Take US Alternate Hwy. 14 west from Burgess Junction to reach FR 14. Follow FR 14 for 3 miles. Bear left at the junction with FR 11 to stay on FR 14. Follow FR 14 for another 5.7 miles to FR 146. Take FR 146. It is a passable road, although you'll have to slow down so much that you can hardly outrun the dust your vehicle kicks up. It is just a short stretch (0.4-mile long) and can easily be walked if the road gets wet and the dust has turned to mud. **Trailhead GPS:** N44 51.471' / W107 54.802'

THE HIKE

A 200-foot waterfall and an abandoned mine wait at the bottom of a short 0.4-mile hike. Following an old mine road, the trail drops 410 feet in elevation to Porcupine Creek within the channel of Devil Canyon. There is a sign at the trailhead reminding visitors to the falls that there is "No Riding or Pack Animals on Trail #135."

The trail weaves down through fir and pine. Careful on the way down, as the footing is unsecure and over loose gravel. I counted about 200 steps creatively

Porcupine Creek

Porcupine Creek

constructed out of wood, stone, and even a few natural roots. Ironically, I counted a few less steps on the way back up, but I was more focused on breathing than counting at that point.

Great slabs of granite rise like blades from the timbered walls of the canyon. The trail bottoms out at a pool at the base of Porcupine Falls. Old mine tailings remind

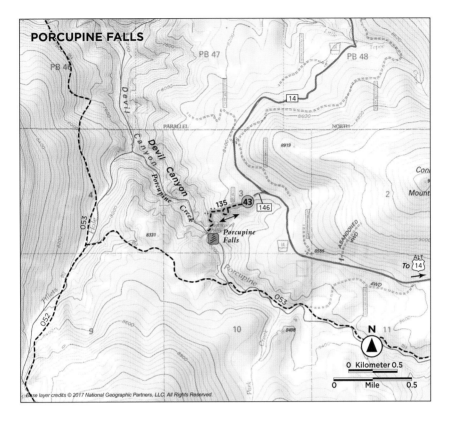

visitors of the history of the early 1900s. Not much remains, but the old mining camp is on the opposite shore and downstream from the falls. Gold miners blasted a diversion channel that remains visible. Here they ran water through the riffle box used to separate the heavy gold from the lighter gravels.

The views of the falls are stunning from the pool below. For another perspective, scramble up the rocks and get a different angle on the falls.

MILES AND DIRECTIONS

0.0   Trailhead.

0.4   Porcupine Falls.

44. MEDICINE WHEEL

WHY GO?

Medicine Wheel National Historic Landmark sits high atop a windswept ridge of Medicine Mountain. This is a sacred site for many Native American tribes.

THE RUNDOWN

Distance: 2.6 miles out-and-back

Elevation gain: 150 feet

Difficulty: Easy due to paved trail surface and moderate distance

Hiking time: About 1 hour

Best seasons: Summer, early fall

Fees and permits: No fees or permits required

Trail contacts: Bighorn National Forest, 2013 Eastside 2nd St., Sheridan, WY 82801, (307) 674-2600, http://www.fs.usda.gov/bighorn

Maps: USDA Forest Service Bighorn National Forest, USGS Medicine Wheel

Dog-friendly: Leashed dogs are permitted

Trail surface: Pavement

Nearest town: Lovell, Wyoming

Other trail users: None

Special considerations: This is a sacred site many Native Americans and is occasionally closed off briefly for private spiritual ceremonies.

FINDING THE TRAILHEAD

 FR 12 takes off to the north from US Hwy. Alternate 14. This solid road journeys past a Federal Aviation Administration Radar Dome reaching the Medicine Wheel/Medicine Mountain National Historic Landmark after 1.7 miles.

Trailhead GPS: N44 49.192' / W107 53.954'

THE HIKE

The 2.6-mile round trip hike is along a paved surface. It is fairly gradual incline, but the 9,500+ foot elevation means this is more than a walk in the park.

Along the ridgetop of Medicine Mountain, this short summer hike takes you to one of the most well-preserved and sacred Native American sites in North America, the Medicine Wheel. Its age remains unknown, although researchers estimate it was built over a period of centuries between 500 and 1,500 years ago. Arriving at the stone structure evokes a sense of wonder and spirituality. The Wheel's diameter is grand, circling nearly 80 feet and encompassing twenty-eight radial spokes.

The spokes are rows of limestone boulders extending from a central stone cairn. Six associated ring-shaped cairns are situated around the perimeter. While its exact use is a mystery, the twenty-eight spokes are thought to represent a sacred number. The same number of poles was used to build roofs of the centuries-old Native American ceremonial Sun Dance lodges, perhaps for the 28 days in a lunar cycle. Various markings within the Wheel line up with the rising of significant stars and constellations, foretelling the arrival of the summer solstice.

Today, thousands of visitors make the 1.5-mile trek to experience the Medicine Wheel. Interpretive rangers greet travelers and help to answer questions about the prehistoric structure. Weather permitting, the site is open mid-June through mid-September with occasional and short periods of closing for ceremonial use. Some travelers choose to leave offerings adorned along the enclosing fence; however, visitors are prohibited from taking artifacts or disturbing the sanctity of the area. There are no facilities along the hike or at the site, so plan your prior stops accordingly. From the trailhead, hikers follow a closed mountain road, open only to vehicles with special permission for handicap access. The journey begins with a mild incline offering panoramic alpine views of the habitats home to elk, moose, black bears, coyotes, eagles, and falcons. Pika can be spotted along the road. Summer wildflowers make a quick appearance in the short window when there's little to no snow.

Medicine Wheel
National Historic Site

As you make trip to the Medicine Wheel, remember that Native American tribes have used the land surrounding the site for at least 7,000 years, making this landmark only one of a series of interrelated sites used as ceremonial areas. Sweat lodges, altars, and other prehistoric trails can be found in the encompassing 23,000 acres. In the spring of 1969, the Medicine Wheel (formerly called the Bighorn Medicine Wheel) was added to the National Register of Historic Places. A year later, it was designated as a National Historic Landmark. Then after several years of discourse, the Forest Service and other government officials met with tribal representatives to sign a Historic Preservation Plan to help manage the use and protection of this ancient structure. The plan required the Forest Service to consult with Native American alliances and coalitions, among other agencies, on any projects within thousands of acres.

When exploring this area, you can't miss the large spherical dome atop nearby Medicine Mountain. This is a radar tower administered by the Federal Aviation Administration.

Medicine Wheel spokes

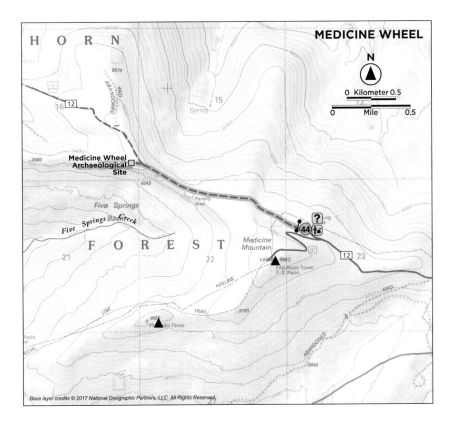

MILES AND DIRECTIONS

0.0 Medicine Wheel Visitor Center.

1.3 Medicine Wheel.

45. **COTTONWOOD CANYON**

WHY GO?

The gap that is Cottonwood Canyon is visible from the west as you approach the Bighorn Mountains from the Bighorn Basin. The transition from desert badlands to mountain forests can be experienced on this steep hike.

THE RUNDOWN

Distance: 8.8 miles out-and-back

Elevation gain: 2,200 feet

Difficulty: Strenuous due to elevation gains, exposed conditions, uneven footing

Hiking time: About 9 hours

Best seasons: Spring, fall

Fees and permits: No fees or permits required

Trail contacts: BLM Cody Field Office, 1002 Blackburn St., Cody,

WY 82414, (307) 578-5900, http://www.blm.gov/wy/st/en/field_offices/Cody.html

Maps: USDA Forest Service Bighorn National Forest, USGS Cottonwood Canyon

Dog-friendly: Dogs must be under control

Trail surface: Uneven terrain

Nearest town: Lovell, Wyoming

Other trail users: Equestrians

FINDING THE TRAILHEAD

Take US Hwy. Alternate 14 east from Lovell. After crossing Bighorn Lake, turn left (north) onto John Blue Road. Take an immediate right onto a rocky but drivable primitive road that leads east for 6 miles to the mouth of Cottonwood Canyon. There is ample parking, as well as pit toilet facilities and livestock watering tanks at the end of the road. The trail follows a closed road to the east as it heads into the canyon.

Trailhead GPS: N44 52.066' / W108 04.274'

THE HIKE

This deep and narrow canyon is a bit of a unique hike for the Bighorn Mountains. It provides a lesson in elevation as it climbs up from the desert basin to the forested slopes of the mountains. Cottonwood Creek is a mere trickle of water for much of the year, although it gains volume during spring runoff and following major rains.

The Bureau of Land Management put in a horse corral, and primitive camping is allowed near the trailhead. The trail begins in stands of juniper a couple tenths of a mile from the mouth of Cottonwood Canyon. Follow the roadbed east from the parking area to the canyon. Here you'll cross through a gate and past a couple of quarries.

The trail climbs as it enters the canyon. Here mountain-mahogany gives the hike a desert scrub feel. Mountain-mahogany is a nitrogen-fixing shrub that can grow on rocky sites with thin soils. This shrub is often a winter food source

Cottonwood Canyon

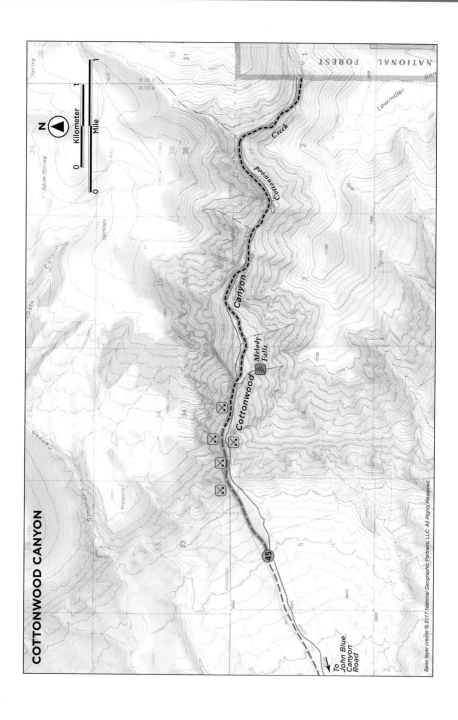

COTTONWOOD CANYON

from mule deer, and the plants respond to heavy browsing by growing more spiny branches.

Look for chukar along this stretch of trail. These gamebirds, native to southern Eurasia, have thrived in the Bighorn Basin since early releases by the Game & Fish Department in the 1930s and 1940s. The first hunting season on them was in 1955. The way the birds scamper upslope will inspire you to add a bit more spring in your own step.

A mile and a half into the hike, after an especially steep climb, pause to take in the contrast between the eastern and western views. Beyond this point, you'll note an increase in conifers. Few cottonwoods are found along Cottonwood Creek, but aspen are more abundant along the riparian corridor.

The trail makes several crossings of Cottonwood Creek as it climbs eastward. Canyon walls line the trail but do little to block out the midday sun. Be prepared for warm temperatures on this exposed walk.

The return hike offers a welcome opportunity to go downhill. The gray and red canyon walls make a nice frame for the vista that extends across the Bighorn Basin to the Absaroka Mountains some 60 miles away.

One could theoretically follow Cottonwood Canyon all the way to the Bighorn National Forest and FR 119. The going gets tough in the upper stretches, however.

MILES AND DIRECTIONS

0.0   Cottonwood Canyon Trailhead.

0.2   Cross a gate and past a couple of gravel pits.

0.5   Ford Cottonwood Creek.

1.2   Canyon narrows. First of many easy stream crossings.

4.0   Canyon forks keep to south, trail becomes especially difficult to follow.

4.4   Bighorn National Forest boundary.

MEDICINE WHEEL AND SURROUNDINGS
ADDITIONAL HIKES

Lodge Grass Trail (Trail 061) is a remote trail beginning on FR 11 and ending at the Wyoming/Montana State Line. The trail can be faint in places, and there is at least one major blow down that you'll have to navigate around. But this route travels through some spectacular landscapes.

Bighorn Canyon National Recreation Area straddles the Wyoming and Montana border just west of the Bighorns. The area offers 28 miles of hiking along 14 trails. *Hiking Wyoming* describes the **Skyes Mountain** hike in further detail. It is a 4-mile round trip effort that is equal parts strenuous and rewarding.

Rainbow Canyon is an off-trail route on Bureau of Land Management lands a few miles west of the Five Springs Campground. Sadly, the parking lot seems to be a hangout for litterbug partiers. However, the canyon itself is a fine example of the Bighorn Basin accentuated by Five Springs and Crystal Creeks.

Petes Hole Trail (Trail 104), off the end of FR 132, offers a stunning view west overlooking the Bighorn Basin and views north to Medicine Mountain. The trail is vague at best in some places, but this is still a neat area to explore.

Bighorn Canyon National Recreation Area offers up great hiking
JARREN KUIPERS

SOUTHWEST BIGHORNS AND BASIN COUNTRY

The Bighorn Basin is an arid landscape sprawling out to the west of the Bighorn Mountains. The area has a southern Utah feel to it in many ways with badland buttes of red, orange, and yellow. Hoodoos stand like statues carved by wind from the sandstone. The painted desert scenery and rugged canyon walls make for unique exploring. Water can be scarce in these parts, and temperatures can soar in the heat of the day. Spring is a great time to explore these parts, as the high country remains nestled under a cloak of snow. This area is critical winter range for elk and mule deer.

Humans have occupied the Bighorn Basin for at least 10,000 years. The Medicine Lodge Archaeological Site offers a glimpse into the lives of past hunters. The short nature loop hike is a great introduction to the region.

Rugged Paint Rock Canyon links the Bighorns from basin to mountain. The creek is a popular destination for trout anglers as well.

You earn your views on the Salt Lick Trail. This hike scales the northern wall of Tensleep Canyon, plateauing out at the Bighorn Basin.

With a population of plus or minus 250 people, Ten Sleep is the hub in the southwest Bighorns. Named because it was ten nights of sleep away from major Sioux camps near the Platte River to the south and near Bridger, Montana, to the north.

Tensleep Canyon is a growing destination for rock climbing. See if you can spot climbers clinging onto the sides of the cliffs as you travel up and down the canyon.

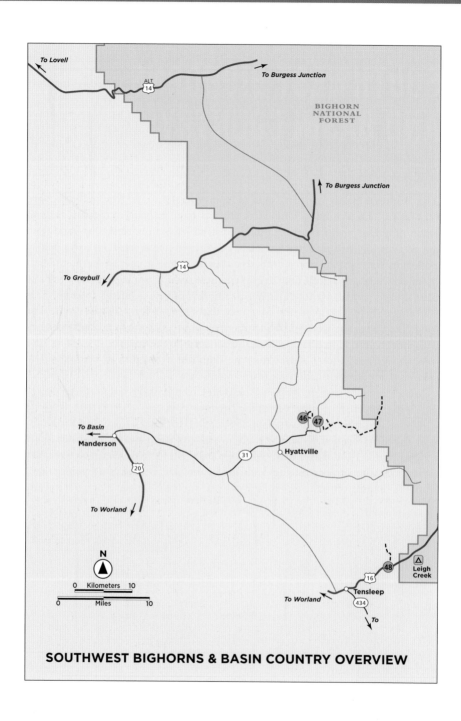

SOUTHWEST BIGHORNS & BASIN COUNTRY OVERVIEW

46. MEDICINE LODGE ARCHAEOLOGICAL SITE

WHY GO?

Medicine Lodge Archaeology Site is known for hundreds of prehistoric petroglyphs and pictographs visible along a 700-foot long sandstone cliff near the parking area. This short loop highlights the human history of the area as well as the natural ecosystems found here.

THE RUNDOWN

Distance: 1-mile loop

Elevation gain: Minimal

Difficulty: Easy due to short distance and flat walking

Hiking time: About 1 hour

Best seasons: Spring, summer, fall

Fees and permits: No fees or permits required

Trail contacts: Medicine Lodge State Archaeological Site, 4800 Rd. 52, Hyattville, WY 82428, (307) 469-2234, http://wyoparks.state.wy.us/Site/SiteInfo.aspx?siteID=25; BLM Worland Field Office, 101 South 23rd St., Worland, WY 82401, (307)

347-5100, http://www.blm.gov/wy/st/en/field_offices/Worland.html

Maps: USDA Forest Service Bighorn National Forest, BLM Worland, USGS Allen Draw, USGS Hyatt Ranch

Dog-friendly: Dogs must be under control

Trail surface: Smooth path, gravel road

Nearest town: Ten Sleep and Manderson, Wyoming

Other trail users: None

Special considerations: Fee camping is available

FINDING THE TRAILHEAD

From the intersection of Wyoming 31 and Lower Nowood Road (east of Manderson and 20 miles north of Ten Sleep), head east on Wyoming 31. In 6.8 miles, at the "T" intersection on the north side of Hyattville, turn left (north) onto Alkali-Cold Springs Road. After 0.3 mile, turn right onto Cold Springs Road. Take Cold Springs Rd. 4.7 miles to the entrance of the Medicine Lodge Archaeological Site. Follow the signs to reach the parking area near the Archaeological Visitor Center.

Trailhead GPS: N44 17.878' / W107 32.508'

Wet Medicine Lodge Creek

THE HIKE

Much research has been done in the Medicine Lodge Archaeological Site region. The most visible artifacts remain in place with hundreds of prehistoric petroglyphs and pictographs visible along a 700-foot long sandstone cliff near the parking area. Digs in the area have unearthed over 10,000 years' worth of human occupation at this site.

In addition to this fascinating history, Medicine Lodge Archaeological Site offers up camping, public horse corrals, a quaint visitor center, and access to some of the most impressive stretches of the Bighorn Basin.

To get a small taste of the unique ecosystems of the area, take the 1-mile Medicine Lodge Nature Trail. This loop trail circles the main grounds of the State Historic Site. It starts at the base of the sandstone cliff easel of prehistoric artists. Then it passes a couple of cabins that host interpretive displays about the local flora and fauna. Especially fascinating is the elk cabin, highlighting the importance of this area as winter range for these stately mammals. Next, the trail crosses Dry Medicine Lodge Creek, which only has water during spring and summer runoff. From here, it approaches the base of Shiprock, a large sandstone outcrop that serves as the divide between Dry and Wet Medicine Lodge Creeks. Hang a right, walk past the Group Area Picnic Shelter, and then reach the confluence of Dry and Wet Medicine Lodge Creeks. Follow the Wet branch, which holds a healthy population of both brown and rainbow trout, back to the main entrance road. Follow the road to the right to return to the visitor center parking area and bathrooms.

Petroglyph Cliff at Medicine Lodge Archaeological Site

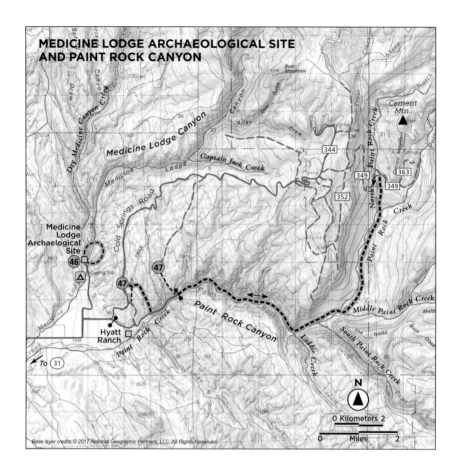

MEDICINE LODGE ARCHAEOLOGICAL SITE
AND PAINT ROCK CANYON

For folks looking for a longer hike, head west from Shiprock. Dry Medicine Lodge Canyon is a few miles up the road, and you can hike this scenic gem to the Bighorn National Forest boundary and beyond. Wet Medicine Lodge Creek is also worth exploring. The Medicine Lodge Wildlife Management Area is closed to motorized travel from Dec 1 to June 30 to protect critical winter range. Foot traffic is allowed year-round to provide fishing access to Medicine Lodge Creek. Both extended hikes represent typical Bighorn Basin habitat. There isn't much trail per se in places. Part of the fun on these hikes is exploring on your own.

MILES AND DIRECTIONS

0.0 Start at Medicine Lodge Archaeological Site parking area.

0.3 Shiprock.

1.0 Return to parking area.

47. **PAINT ROCK CANYON TRAIL**

WHY GO?

Paint Rock Canyon explores an impressive canyon along the western slopes of the Bighorn Mountains. Starting along the badlands of the Bighorn Basin near Medicine Lodge Archaeological Site, the trail follows picturesque Paint Rock Creek east to the border of the Bighorn National Forest.

THE RUNDOWN   See map on page 226.

Distance: 18.8 miles out-and-back to Forest Service boundary

Difficulty: Moderate due to distance and uneven trail

Elevation gain: 2,345 feet

Hiking time: About 9 hours

Best seasons: Late spring, early fall

Fees and permits: No fees or permits required

Trail contacts: BLM Worland Field Office, 101 South 23rd St., Worland, WY 82401, (307) 347-5100, http://www.blm.gov/wy/st/en/field_offices/Worland.html

Maps: USDA Forest Service Bighorn National Forest, BLM Worland, USGS Hyatt Ranch, USGS Bush Butte

Dog-friendly: Dogs must be under control

Trail surface: Uneven terrain, gravel road

Nearest town: Ten Sleep and Manderson, Wyoming

Other trail users: None

Special considerations: Private Land Crossing closed Oct 1–May 10.

FINDING THE TRAILHEAD

From the intersection of Wyoming 31 and Lower Nowood Road (14 miles east of Manderson and 20 miles north of Ten Sleep), head east on Wyoming 31. In 6.8 miles, at the "T" intersection on the north side of Hyattville, turn left (north) onto Alkali-Cold Springs Road. After 0.3 mile, turn right onto Cold Springs Road. Take Cold Springs Road about 5 miles, passing the entrance to Medicine Lodge Archaeological Site along the way. The trailhead is less than a mile after Cold Springs Road makes a turn to the left (north) and heads up a hill. A sign marks the Paint Rock Canyon Parking area on the left (west) side of the road. The trailhead is opposite the parking area to the east of Cold Springs Road.

A second access from the Lone Tree Trail is about 5.5 miles farther along Cold Springs Road. Signs point out the primitive road heading south for 3 miles to the trailhead. This rough road is heavily rutted and along a steep grade. You can probably walk it faster than you can drive it.

Trailhead GPS: N44 16.961' / W107 31.046' or N44 17.556' / W107 29.580'

THE HIKE

There are two trailhead options on the western end of this hike. The main access point is from Cold Spring Road. From here, the trail crosses a private section of the Hyatt Ranch before continuing along BLM lands. Access is allowed from May 11 to Sept 30. A year-round access option is from the Lone Tree Trail.

Paint Rock Canyon Trailhead

This trail starts 3 miles off of Cold Springs Road at the bottom of a miserable and slow traveling two-track.

From the Cold Springs Road parking area, cross the road to find the trailhead at a marked gate. Respect the landowner and keep gates as you found them. Stick to the trail and the dirt road as you travel over private property, passing irrigated hayfields and pasturelands.

As the Paint Rock Canyon walls rise, the trail crosses a fence to return to BLM lands. Lone Tree Trail enters from the north near here as well. The cliff walls reach higher the deeper you penetrate into the canyon.

The next 6 miles offer smooth traveling along a gradual but steady climb. Paint Rock Creek is a substantial body of water choked full of large boulders. Fishing can be solid, but you'll have to work harder to entice the 12–16 inch brown and rainbow trout. These aren't mountain brookies after all.

North and Middle Paint Rock Creeks come together to form Paint Rock Creek just west of the Forest Service boundary. The main trail bends north, merges with the Lower Paint Rock Motorized Trail (Trail 548), and terminates at FR 349 near Cement Mountain. It's possible to bushwhack along Middle Paint Rock to reach National Forest Trail 849. It is a nonmotorized trail on the western end, but eventually turns to an ATV trail that leads to the Battle Park Trailhead.

Unfortunately, cheatgrass can be expected in the Paint Rock Canyon area during the summer season. Summer hiking can be quite hot on this exposed trail, although a refreshing dip in the creek is always an option. Fishing for browns can pick up during the fall. This region provides critical winter range for elk and mule deer.

MILES AND DIRECTIONS

0.0   Paint Rock Canyon Trailhead.

2.0   Trail reaches Hyatt Ranch Road. Turn left and follow road east.

3.2   Road enters BLM land.

7.3   Head of Paint Rock Canyon.

8.5   Bridge over Paint Rock Creek. Follow trail north along main for Paint Rock Creek.

9.9   Trail enters Bighorn National Forest.

48. **SALT LICK TRAIL**

WHY GO?

This trail offers up an impressive perspective above Tensleep Canyon and a view of the western slopes of the Bighorns.

THE RUNDOWN

Distance: 6.9 miles out-and-back

Elevation gain/loss: 888 feet

Difficulty: Moderate due to steep climb, uneven footing, and moderate distance

Hiking time: About 4 hours

Best seasons: Spring

Fees and permits: No fees or permits required

Trail contacts: BLM Worland Field Office, 101 South 23rd St., Worland, WY 82401, (307)

347-5100, http://www.blm.gov/wy/st/en/field_offices/Worland.html

Maps: USDA Forest Service Bighorn National Forest, BLM Worland, USGS Old Maid Gulch

Dog-friendly: Dogs must be under control

Trail surface: Uneven terrain, boulders, steps

Nearest town: Ten Sleep, Wyoming

Other trail users: Equestrians

FINDING THE TRAILHEAD

From Ten Sleep head east on US Hwy. 16 for 6.5 miles to the well-marked trailhead. Parking and the trail are on the north side of the highway.
Trailhead GPS: N44 04.226' / W107 20.920'

THE HIKE

The trailhead is well marked off of US Hwy. 16, 6.5 miles east of Ten Sleep. The steepness of this hike is unavoidable, and it looms directly overhead. It is also worth noting that this hike is pretty exposed and doesn't have any water access. Don't let these facts derail you though. It's a pretty incredible experience to peer over the edge of Tensleep Canyon. The hike is on Bureau of Land Management lands and is open year-round. The surrounding Carter/Billy Miles Public Access Area, however, is checkerboarded throughout and is closed for much of the year. These areas offer up seasonal access for hunting from Sept 1 to Dec 31.

The big sagebrush near the parking lot quickly transitions to stands of juniper. The instant and constant elevation gains provide ample justification for plenty of rest stops to take in the evermore impressive views.

The trail is like a two-handled lollipop with stems on opposite ends of a short loop. The sign at the trailhead reminds folks that the eastern section of the loop has some rocky sections and makeshift steps that are unsuitable for horses. If you aren't paying attention to each step you take, they could potentially be unsuitable for humans as well. The western section, about two-thirds of the loop, winds around the cliff face before reaching to the top. From here, expect ridiculous views of Tensleep Canyon and the Wigwam Fish Rearing Station nearly 400 feet below. You'll hike through some ponderosa pines as the two sections of the loop come back together.

North of the loop, the trail can be a little faint in places. You can continue northish for 2.5 miles until you reach South Brokenback Road (Rd. 1415). You'll hike through some stands of juniper. Take note of the blackened skeletons of some of the juniper, remnants from past fires.

The trail takes a bit of a dogleg to the west, and then it crosses Salt Lick Creek. Much to my amazement, there was even a mineral block salt lick at the edge of creek, a reminder that cattle graze this rangeland during some parts of the year. After you hop over the thin green riparian corridor, you'll head up the opposite bank. Upon crossing through the gate (if it's closed, close it again behind you), keep to the right to continue on the remaining mile to South Brokenback Road.

Tensleep Canyon from Salt Lick Trail

All along the hike, prominent buttes stand out in the foreground. To the east, the Bighorns loom beyond. Turning west, on a clear day, you can see all the way to the Absaroka Mountains across the Bighorn Basin. Don't just look up though. Looking down you might spot a horny toad (officially eastern short-horned lizard) scampering amongst the black sage or anywhere along this stretch of trail.

You could simply hike the 1.6-mile lollipop loop, but if you did that, you'd miss out on the great 2.5-mile stretch of walking along the red dirt and badlands that flank the western end of the Bighorns.

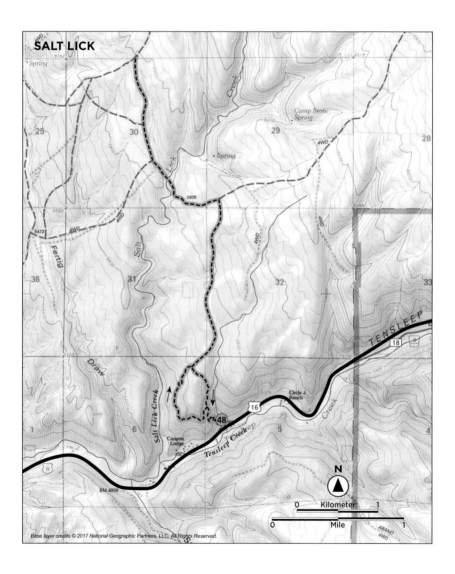

This trail receives highest pressure during the fall hunting season, but it makes for a unique experience and shouldn't be overlooked during the rest of the year. And after a somewhat strenuous hike such as this, you owe yourself a visit to the nearby Ten Sleep Brewing Company 8 miles down the road.

MILES AND DIRECTIONS

0.0 Salt Lick Trail Trailhead.

0.3 Start of loop, go left.

1.2 Junction. Go left for longer hike or right to close loop and return to trailhead.

2.8 Cross Salt Lick Creek.

3.7 Trail reaches South Brokenback Road. Turn around (you'll retrace steps 2.5 miles back to loop.)

4.6 Cross Salt Lick Creek again.

6.2 Return to junction at loop, go left. (Right retraces steps back to trailhead.)

6.6 Close the loop. Turn left to return to trailhead.

6.9 Salt Lick Trail Trailhead.

SOUTHWEST BIGHORNS AND BASIN COUNTRY ADDITIONAL HIKES

Dry Medicine Lodge Creek and **Medicine Lodge Canyon** both offer wilderness hiking adventures in deep canyon bottoms. The lower reaches come out at the Medicine Lodge Archaeological Site. Upper stretches are off of FR 17 near Spanish Point and off of Cold Springs Road near Captain Jack Draw, respectively.

The **Tensleep Preserve**, located southeast of Ten Sleep, is a research and educational preserve operated by The Nature Conservancy. Limited access is provided for hikers from May to Oct. Contact The Nature Conservancy for more information.

HIKE INDEX